The Revd Dr David Owen is a minister in the United Reformed Church, now retired and living in Broad Haven, Pembrokeshire. His pastorates were at Glyn Church, Risca, Richmond Hill, Bournemouth, Reigate Park, Surrey and the Landsker Group in Pembrokeshire. He served two short exchange ministries in the USA at Dallas and Seattle.

During his Surrey pastorate of 28 years he was also a hospital chaplain and teacher of religious studies. He has led Christian worship broadcasts, and was often involved in programmes for commercial radio.

David Owen is the author of several books (including one of 70 hymns), and wrote the religious article for *Woman's Weekly* magazine over a period of nine years, reaching a readership of millions. He was a regular writer of Bible study, sermon and leaders' notes for the International Bible Reading Association.

LIVING THROUGH BEREAVEMENT

*With the help of Christian
thought and prayer*

David M. Owen

First published in Great Britain in 2008

Society for Promoting Christian Knowledge
36 Causton Street
London SW1P 4ST

British Library Cataloguing-in-Publication Data
A catalogue record for this book is available from the British Library

ISBN 978-0-281-05934-8

1 3 5 7 9 10 8 6 4 2

Typeset by Graphicraft Limited, Hong Kong
Printed in Great Britain by Ashford Colour Press

Produced on paper from sustainable forests

Contents

Preface   vii

1   Death and the life after: What the Bible teaches   1

2   The concept of the soul   21

3   Death no stranger   30

4   Fear and faith   35

5   This life in preparation   43

6   Too soon to die   50

7   Unable to bear it   67

8   Coping with disaster   74

9   The cost of war   85

10 Solace in grief   97

11 Our living Lord   116

12 Heaven awaits   126

13 Together for ever   132

14 The eternal company   136

Sources and acknowledgements   140

*Dedicated to
my wife Margaret,
whose death left an aching loneliness,
but also a greater understanding of those
who suffer the pain of bereavement*

Preface

Life from birth to death consists of attachments and detachments, gains and losses. Birth itself separates us from our mother's body; in the following years we form relationships with our parents, loved ones, friends and countless others whom we meet. We receive an education, qualify for a career, acquire possessions, and develop a personal character and religious faith. But just as commonly we experience detachments; we lose loved ones and friends, we change or lose jobs, we suffer ill-health and setbacks, part with material things, and in the end death brings about the irrevocable detachment of our earthly ties.

Job in the Old Testament struck a note of appreciation and realism: 'The Lord gives and the Lord takes away; blessed be the name of the Lord' (Job 1.21 NEB). All too often our losses overwhelm us, we dwell on them and succumb to self-pity, we turn against God and forget to be grateful for all we have received and still possess, by which our lives are blessed.

There is 'a time to lose', said the writer of Ecclesiastes (3.6 NEB). If by those words he meant that most painful of losses we suffer through the death of a dear one, he does us a service by reminding us of its inevitability, for we can easily take our closest relationships for granted and be unprepared for the sorrow of parting. Bereavement is unavoidable if we love someone, and we know this, yet it can take us unawares, leave us shattered, and linger a long time before we experience recovery.

Bereavement means to be deprived of something or someone valued, especially through death. As a church minister and hospital chaplain I was frequently called upon to help bereaved people, and few weeks went by without a funeral service. The majority of occasions one could describe as 'normal', that is the death of someone elderly after a long and useful life. But while there was reason to celebrate so many years, that life was often deeply mourned by those closest, giving meaning to our saying that the longer they are with us, the more they are missed. I know a woman who grieved deeply for her mother who had died aged 99. On the other hand there are those plunged into grief by the death of someone much younger, and especially devastating is the loss of a child or young adult. Every person's bereavement varies according to circumstances – the closeness of the relationship, the age of the one who has died and the manner of their dying, and one's own ability to cope. And all would agree that bereavement, though common to us all, is a sore wounding which takes time to heal. But with help it does heal.

The death of my wife was 'normal' in terms of her age, but however 'experienced' I might have been, her death left me deeply bereaved and lonely. She was the dearest wife a man could have, my soulmate, best friend and helper over 45 years, and for the first time I confess I came to know grief at its most heart-rending. Its intense pain had come home at last.

Out of that, and a longer pastoral involvement, has emerged this book. I know that bereaved people are helped by reflecting on what others have written; I certainly have been. So I hope that *Living Through Bereavement* will serve this purpose. It is largely a sequel to my previous *Losing and Living* which considered other losses too, such as good health, employment, pets and possessions. This book looks only at bereavement following the death of a loved one, in whatever circumstances. It uses some material from the previous book and adds more – all designed to help us through our loss and to reflect on the Christian message of comfort, restoration, and of the hope held out to us by our resurrected Lord of life beyond this life.

I am most grateful to SPCK for publishing this work, to my editor Alison Barr for her hard work in editing the material, and to Steve Gove, Sally Green and the rest of the team at SPCK.

David Maldwyn Owen

1

Death and the life after
What the Bible teaches

———◆—◆◆———

The Old Testament

Strange though it may seem, the Old Testament does not give us that certainty of belief in the after-life which we might expect. This is not to devalue the Old Testament, of course, but it means that we must be careful to see it in its correct time setting and prevailing social-theological environment. The religion of the Hebrews was very much a religion for the present world, and God was thought to have little jurisdiction over other domains. He was said to reward the righteous in this life with health and prosperity, and to expel the unrighteous to Sheol.

Sheol was imagined to be a great hollow cavern beneath the earth (hell as a place 'down under' derives from this). It was not so much a place of physical torture – that idea came later – but of separation from God. Sheol was outside God's jurisdiction. To be cut off from communion with God was something the Hebrews regarded as the worst punishment of all. It was only later, when they believed in God as the universal Creator, that he was thought to be present everywhere and that his mercy reached Sheol itself.

Gradually the long-held view that God rewards the righteous with long life and prosperity in this world ceased to ring true. A good man could suffer ill-health and misfortune and die prematurely, whereas a God-less man might continue to prosper for many years, so what results could the righteous expect, and when, and where?

There is little direct expression in the teaching of the prophets concerning the after-life, but the assumptions contained in their demands for justice for all are most convincing. It was felt that surely the ultimate fate of those who remain faithful to God, not least those who are martyrs for his sake, must be different from the God-less and the ruthless who put his servants to death. If God is a good God there must be a moral law which makes justice effective, if not in this life, then surely in the next! So a more positive belief grew. And as man discovered more about God and enjoyed increasing communion with him, it became more and more unthinkable that such enjoyment should cease at death.

It is, however, only as we come to the last four hundred years of the Old Testament period that immortal longings take more positive shape. The Book of Job, which wrestles with the problem of suffering and a God of love, was written probably about 400 BC. In it we hear what appears to be a clear expression of belief in life after death:

> For I know that my Redeemer lives, and at last he will stand upon the earth; and after my skin has been thus destroyed, then without my flesh I shall see God.
>
> Job 19.25–26 RSV

What exactly Job meant by seeing God 'without my flesh', and whether this was to be in this life or after death, we are not sure, but there is no doubt that Job has reached the climax of his agony, and out of utter despair asserts his conviction that life cannot end in this tragic way and that God will not fail him. While we cannot say for certain that these words express the doctrine of immortality, they do contain the germ of the idea which was soon to become widespread among Jewish, and later among Christian believers.

The Book of Daniel, written about 170 BC, gives us a most definite belief in the after-life:

> Many of those who sleep in the dust of the earth will wake, some to everlasting life and some to the reproach of eternal abhorrence.   Daniel 12.2 NEB

This teaching is a noticeable feature of the Apocrypha, that is, the books written during the period 300 BC–AD 100, the period before the definite separation of the Church from Judaism. These books were received by the early Church as part of the Greek version of the Old Testament, but they were not included in the Hebrew Bible as such.

In Second Maccabees we read of a woman who witnessed her seven sons die as martyrs for their faith, but she was confident that death was not the end for them:

> It is the Creator of the universe who moulds man at his birth and plans the origin of all things. Therefore he, in his mercy, will give back life and breath again . . .
>   2 Maccabees 7.23 NEB

The wisdom of Solomon, written one hundred years before Jesus was born, expresses hope in the after-life and rewards for the righteous in no uncertain terms. The philosophy, 'eat, drink and be merry, for tomorrow we die', is that of the pagan:

> Death is not king on earth, for justice is immortal.
>   Wisdom of Solomon 1.14 NEB

> But God created man for immortality, and made him the image of his own eternal self.
>   Wisdom of Solomon 2.23 NEB

Actual length of life is no longer seen as the reward of the religious man, for the righteous may die prematurely:

> But the good man, even if he dies an untimely death, will be at rest. For it is not length of life and number of years

which bring the honour due to age . . . Even after his death the just man will shame the godless who are still alive . . . Men will see the wise man's end, without understanding what the Lord had purposed for him and why he took him into safe keeping.

Wisdom of Solomon 4.7, 8, 16, 17 NEB

The writer sums up his belief in words that have now become familiar to us:

But the souls of the just are in God's hand, and torment shall not touch them. In the eyes of foolish men they seemed to be dead; their departure was reckoned as defeat, and their going from us as disaster. But they are at peace, for though in the sight of men they may be punished, they have sure hope of immortality . . . Those who have put their trust in him shall understand that he is true, and the faithful shall attend upon him in love; they are his chosen, and grace and mercy shall be theirs.

Wisdom of Solomon 3.1—4.9 NEB

But the just live for ever; their reward is in the Lord's keeping, and the Most High has them in his care. Therefore royal splendour shall be theirs, and a fair diadem from the Lord himself; he will protect them with his right hand and shield them with his arm.

Wisdom of Solomon 5.15–16 NEB

We close our look at the Old Testament with some well-known and well-loved passages that tell of man's longing for continuing communion with God; his belief that the God who is perfect love will be with him, always and everywhere:

. . . my spirit rejoices,
my body too rests unafraid;

for thou wilt not abandon me to Sheol
nor suffer thy faithful servant to see the pit.
Thou wilt show me the path of life;
in thy presence is the fullness of joy,
in thy right hand pleasures for evermore.

Psalm 16.9b–11 NEB

The Lord *is* my shepherd; I shall not want.
He maketh me to lie down in green pastures; he leadeth
me beside the still waters.
He restoreth my soul: he leadeth me in the paths of
righteousness for his name's sake.
Yea, though I walk through the valley of the shadow of
death, I will fear no evil: for thou *art* with me; thy rod
and thy staff they comfort me.
Thou preparest a table before me in the presence of mine
enemies: thou anointest my head with oil; my cup
runneth over.
Surely goodness and mercy shall follow me all the days of
my life: and I will dwell in the house of the LORD for
ever.

Psalm 23 AV

. . . I am always with thee,
thou holdest my right hand;
thou dost guide me by thy counsel
and afterwards wilt receive me with glory.
Whom have I in heaven but thee?
And having thee, I desire nothing else on earth.
Though heart and body fail,
yet God is my possession for ever.

Psalm 73.23–26 NEB

Bless the LORD, my soul;
my innermost heart, bless his holy name . . .

Man's days are like the grass;
he blossoms like the flowers of the field:
a wind passes over them, and they cease to be,
and their place knows them no more.
But the LORD's love never fails those who fear him;
his righteousness never fails their sons and their grandsons
who listen to his voice and keep his covenant,
    who remember his commandments and obey them.

Psalm 103.1, 15–18 NEB

The New Testament

In turning to the New Testament we take a great step forward
in our understanding of the after-life. Indeed, we can confidently speak of the New Testament as 'The Book of Life', for
it tells of life in this world and beyond this world – life with a
capital L.

The New Testament makes the astounding claim that the
struggles and aspirations of God's people in the Old Testament
reach their fulfilment in the life, death and resurrection of Jesus
Christ who is heralded as God's Messiah. It is this claim that
distinguishes Christianity. Clearly then, if we are to be guided
and strengthened in our belief in life after death, we must look
at the teaching and experience of Jesus, the impact he made on
his own followers and on the early Christian Church.

Jesus told of death and resurrection

In his life and ministry Jesus came face to face with the fact
of death. It is generally accepted that his earthly father Joseph
died when Jesus was a youth, so he would have known sorrow
within his own family and the responsibility that falls upon
the eldest son. He knew too what it was like to lose a friend:
on the death of Lazarus we are told that Jesus wept – and how
much that tells us about him! We find that he mingled with
mourners in their homes, and we read of a few occasions when

he restored the dead to life. Jesus talked a great deal about death, though never in a morbid way. He took for granted the fact of natural death and therefore said little about it, whereas his main concern lay with the deaths of his faithful followers and his own impending death. He warned his disciples that they would die for their faith, but promised that their courage and perseverance would bring them salvation and result in the furtherance of his kingdom. Anyone who wished to become his disciple 'must leave self behind; day after day he must take up his cross, and come with me' (Luke 9.23 NEB), but such denial of one's life in this world would gain eternal life. He talked about the necessity of a grain of wheat dying in the ground in order to produce fruit (John 12.24–25).

His warnings were, of course, related to his own forthcoming death, which he saw as a necessary fulfilment of his divine purpose to surrender his life as 'a ransom for many'. He looked upon his death as a 'cup' which he would drink, and in the Garden of Gethsemane he prayed that the 'cup' might pass from him; so great was his love of life and so much did he dread the prospect of crucifixion. He also saw his death as a 'baptism' and we know that baptism symbolizes the start of a new life. When he spoke about the departure he was to fulfil in Jerusalem, and when we realize that the basic meaning of 'departure' was 'exodus', we can see that Jesus intended his death to be a victory march from bondage to freedom.

Quite clearly Jesus expected his own resurrection. Several times he repeated the prediction that he would be rejected by the Jewish authorities, put to death, and that 'three days afterwards he will rise again' (Mark 10.34 NEB) – a phrase implying a definite act of resurrection and not some vague ethereal survival. His resurrection would create a new form of life, and give a new power of life to all believers. As God's committed people they would reap the benefits of his resurrection; they would come from all parts of the world and dine at the great Messianic banquet (Matthew 8.11; Luke 13.29).

The Gospels of Matthew, Mark and Luke each record a fairly detailed encounter Jesus had with the Sadducees concerning the resurrection. The Sadducees, the rigid and legalistic religious class, denied belief in the resurrection of the dead. In his argument with them Jesus shows how the resurrection is asserted in the Old Testament itself. Even the Patriarchs, said Jesus, though they have been physically dead for many centuries, are still in fellowship with God, for God is not the God of the dead but of the living (Matthew 22.23–33; Mark 12.18–27; Luke 20.27–40).

The awkward issue which the Sadducees raised concerned a woman who had been married several times – whose wife would she be in the resurrection? Jesus' reply indicates that the nature of the after-life is more all-loving and all-embracing than the life we live on earth. At the same time, of course, it remains intensely personal, for the God with whom we enter into a personal relationship here continues that relationship, and enables us to enjoy to the full all personal relationships with others.

Jesus is resurrected from death

The resurrection of Jesus is the focal point of the New Testament. All the events of his life lead up to it, and it is the heart of the Church's preaching. Without the resurrection, Jesus would have been no more than remembered as a good man, albeit the best of men, who died a martyr's death; instead he founded the great Christian religion which has survived the most impossible odds to become, after two thousand years, the world's major faith. His resurrection gave birth to the Church which, for all its faults, has overcome the pressures of the centuries and is stronger today than ever.

The terrified disciples came together after the resurrection because they were convinced that Jesus was alive. The apostle selected to succeed Judas was to join the others as a witness to the resurrection (Acts 1.22); the central affirmation of the

Pentecost message was that Jesus who had been crucified was alive again, as many were able to testify (Acts 2.32). Clearly then the resurrection was the key event, and to this day Christianity proclaims its stupendous truth. We affirm in the Apostles' Creed that Jesus was 'crucified, dead, and buried . . . the third day he rose again from the dead.'

There is little scope in this book to go into the considerable evidence available to support our Lord's resurrection – we must read elsewhere for that. Sufficient here to say that it has been examined from every conceivable viewpoint, even by the most ardent sceptics and cynics, and no one seems able to refute its validity. Only an event as astounding as the resurrection could have caused such a turning point in the world's history, and it is totally absurd to imagine that for two thousand years the millions of followers of Jesus have been misled.

If any New Testament references are to be made to Jesus' resurrection they must include Paul's thorough treatment of it in the fifteenth chapter of his first letter to the Corinthians. The following selected verses show clearly how the resurrection of Jesus was the central theme of Paul's preaching, and they will be a help to us as we seek to strengthen our own faith:

> Now if this is what we proclaim, that Christ was raised from the dead, how can some of you say there is no resurrection of the dead? If there be no resurrection, then Christ was not raised; and if Christ was not raised, then our gospel is null and void, and so is your faith . . . For if the dead are not raised, it follows that Christ was not raised; and if Christ was not raised, your faith has nothing in it . . .
>
> But the truth is, Christ was raised to life . . . As in Adam all die, so in Christ all will be brought to life . . . This perishable being must be clothed with the imperishable, and what is mortal must be clothed with immortality. And when our mortality has been clothed with immortality, then the saying of Scripture will come true:

'Death is swallowed up; victory is won!' 'O Death, where is your victory? O Death, where is your sting?' . . . God be praised, he gives us the victory through our Lord Jesus Christ.

> 1 Corinthians 15.12–14, 16–17, 20, 23, 53–55, 57 NEB

And let us remind ourselves of Jesus' own outstanding claim:

I am the resurrection and I am life. If a man has faith in me, even though he die, he shall come to life; and no one who is alive and has faith shall ever die.

> John 11.25–26 NEB

Jesus told of judgement to come

Jesus requires of those of us who follow him the highest stand-ard of life we can possibly live, and he is available through his Spirit to help us. It follows from this that there must be a judgement or a reckoning when our day here is complete. Of course, our faulty lives are daily judged by his perfection, and in that way we are being better prepared for life in his nearer presence, but there is certainly an indication of judgement to come in his teachings, as indeed, in the later teachings of Paul.

Jesus wanted his disciples to get rid of stumbling-blocks in this life lest they result in their downfall later (Mark 9.43). In his judgement parables, 'The Wheat and the Tares' (Matthew 13.24–30) and 'The Sheep and the Goats' (Matthew 25.31–46), he said that there would be a process of sorting out in the resurrection.

There is, according to Jesus, only one unforgivable sin, and that is sin against the Holy Spirit. This we understand to mean the sin which so warps a man's spiritual discernment that he is unable to distinguish good from evil, and so cuts himself off from fellowship with God. The signs of this sin are complete lovelessness and an unwillingness to forgive others, and there is a sense in which it is not so much God who has judged this man but the man who has judged himself and brought about his own condemnation. Indeed, this ought to help us understand the meaning of the term 'hell'. It is possible for a man to cut himself off from communion with God and thereby to make his own hell; God has no need to punish him for he is suffering the punishment of his own making. On reflection, it is a comfort to know that all other sins are forgivable, and an equal comfort to be told that God did not send Jesus into the world to judge it, 'but that through him the world might be saved' (John 3.17 NEB). Jesus gives us ample opportunities to learn of him and to walk in his ways. He once declared:

> In very truth, anyone who gives heed to what I say and puts his trust in him who sent me has hold of eternal life, and does not come up for judgement, but has already passed from death to life.   John 5.24 NEB

One of the finest examples of forgiving love was displayed by Jesus himself from the cross. Not only did he ask God to forgive those who had crucified him, he also turned to a penitent thief and assured him: 'Today you shall be with me in paradise' (Luke 23.43 NEB).

What a consolation it is then to know that God, who has so marvellously shown his love to all people in Jesus, will be there at the gate of death to meet us and those who belong to us. Of course he is bound to judge each of us, and it is right that he should, but we can be quite sure that his judgement will be exercised in mercy. Obviously some people will be more spiritually advanced than others, and they will be rewarded accordingly, but what we know of God's love tells us we can anticipate not only judgement, but forgiveness and renewed opportunities.

Jesus spoke about heaven

The New Testament inherits the traditional Jewish idea of heaven as the dwelling of God and his angelic company. Jesus is said to have descended from heaven and to have returned in the ascension, where he is enthroned with God. It is from heaven that the Holy Spirit is said to have come, and in heaven the faithful departed have their abode.

Quite clearly we are struggling with words to describe the indescribable, and it is most important that we realize this, otherwise we shall stumble over crude literalism. Jesus' references to heaven and the 'kingdom of heaven' are too numerous to mention here; indeed, the bulk of his teaching, which is in parables, is about God's kingdom, God's universal rule. While this has an unmistakably social and present-world emphasis, it certainly has to do with the kingdom beyond this world – God's undisputed and perfect reign in heaven.

We get the gist of his teaching in the following passages:

> Store up treasure in heaven, where there is no moth and no rust to spoil it, no thieves to break in and steal. For where your treasure is, there will your heart be also.
> Matthew 6.20 NEB

> . . . what you should rejoice over is . . . that your names are enrolled in heaven.   Luke 10.20 NEB

> Accept it [persecution] with gladness and exultation, for you have a rich reward in heaven . . .
> Matthew 5.12 NEB

> There are many dwelling-places in my Father's house; if it were not so I should have told you; for I am going there on purpose to prepare a place for you. And if I go and prepare a place for you, I shall come again and receive you to myself, so that where I am you may be also.
> John 14.2–3 NEB

This last reference is one of the loveliest of Jesus' statements about heaven and the after-life. Some of us may be more familiar with the Authorized Version rendering, 'many mansions',

but it is easy to see how this suggests a heaven of stately buildings and posh apartments! Some have suggested the idea of
'resting-places' or 'lay-bys', meaning that in heaven we are
journeying on toward a greater knowledge of God, and that we
need to rest periodically to take stock. There is undoubtedly a
great truth here. We must all have opportunities for realizing
our potential to the full and discovering more of the nature of
God than ever we have been able to do here. Heaven knows
nothing of sorrows and handicaps, and we shall be free to journey on and on.

Others tell us that 'mansions' really indicate that heaven is
so spacious, there is room for all; that the world may close many
doors upon us, but in heaven we shall never be shut out; that
there are no restrictions, no segregation, for the Father's house
has a welcome for everyone. In the immensity of God's love
there is a 'dwelling-place' prepared for all.

Jesus offered a new quality of life

The terms we sometimes use, like 'immortality' and 'everlasting life', may not necessarily bring us the hope and comfort
we need. The idea that at death we merely enter an existence
of endless and purposeless duration is far removed from the
teaching of Christianity – indeed, it is a more pagan view. So
also is the notion of endless sleep.

What Jesus offers is *quality* much more than *quantity*. It must
be more than a question of duration since in the life beyond
death we are in a realm totally outside our present-day narrow
concepts of time. The highest expression of this life of insuper-
able quality is 'eternal life'. In the Gospel of John we read:

> God loved the world so much that he gave his only Son,
> that everyone who has faith in him may not die but have
> eternal life.   John 3.16 NEB

> This is eternal life: to know thee who alone art truly God,
> and Jesus Christ whom thou hast sent.   John 17.3 NEB

. . . whoever drinks the water that I shall give him will never
suffer thirst any more. The water that I shall give him will
be an inner spring always welling up for eternal life.

                                                    John 4.14 NEB

In truth, in very truth I tell you, the believer possesses eternal life. I am the bread of life.   John 6.47–48 NEB

According to the words Jesus used in prayer to his Father, and
which we have just read (John 17.3), eternal life is knowing God,
and knowing Jesus whom God has sent. In biblical terms, 'to
know' means to enjoy a personal experience of, and communion with, God and it is this capacity which distinguishes
a human being from all other animal creatures. We are self-
conscious beings and are able to respond to God's gift of eternal life. We are more than animals desiring earthly, physical
fulfilment, and it is for our higher fulfilment that God makes
his offer to us of eternal life. Jesus said:

I have come that men may have life, and may have it in
all its fullness.   John 10.10 NEB

So we can confidently anticipate a life of unimaginable quality when we leave our earthly abode, but we must also remember that 'eternal life' is not only a future hope; we may
experience something of it here and now. Jesus tells us that the
believer possesses eternal life (John 6.47). This is a great challenge to us then to seek communion with God and to grow up
spiritually during our earthly life, for this present life is our training time, our apprenticeship.

   Eternal life will certainly mean activity rather than endless
sleep or rest. An eternity of doing nothing is quite a terrifying
thought. No, just as God calls us to activity here, so in the life
to come he will engage us in what we can only believe will be
uninterrupted progress in doing his will and discovering the
endless wonder of his love.

Elsewhere in the New Testament

We have already seen how the resurrection of Jesus and the certainty of life after death became the prominent declaration of the Apostles and the early Church. Christians had found a joy so exhilarating that they were prepared to put their own lives at stake – and many did. During the long years of opposition and persecution it was noticeable that these Christians were fearless in the face of the enemy, defending their faith in Jesus Christ as Lord, knowing that his presence and power were with them and in them. Death held no threat because Jesus had conquered death and would grant them victory also.

The following passages from the letters of the New Testament and the Book of Revelation summarize the faith and proclamation of those early years of Christianity. All, except the first passage and the quotations from Hebrews, 1 Peter and the Book of Revelation, are taken from the letters of St Paul:

> The Jesus we speak of has been raised by God, as we can all bear witness . . . Let all Israel then accept as certain that God has made this Jesus, whom you crucified, both Lord and Messiah.   Acts 2.32, 36 NEB

> It is Christ – Christ who died, and, more than that, was raised from the dead – who is at God's right hand, and indeed pleads our cause. Then what can separate us from the love of Christ? Can affliction or hardship? Can persecution, hunger, nakedness, peril or the sword? 'We are being done to death for thy sake all day long,' as Scripture says; 'we have been treated like sheep for slaughter' – and yet in spite of all, overwhelming victory is ours through him who loved us. For I am convinced that there is nothing in death or life, in the realm of spirits or superhuman powers, in the world as it is or the world as it shall be, in the forces of the universe, in heights or depths – nothing in all creation that can separate us from the love of God in Christ Jesus our Lord.   Romans 8.34–39 NEB

I speak God's hidden wisdom, his secret purpose framed
from the very beginning to bring us to our full glory
. . . in the words of Scripture, 'Things beyond our seeing,
things beyond our hearing, things beyond our imagining,
all prepared by God for those who love him', these it is
that God has revealed to us through the Spirit.

1 Corinthians 2.7, 9–10 NEB

. . . for we know that he who raised the Lord Jesus to life
will with Jesus raise us too, and bring us to his presence,
and you with us . . .

No wonder we do not lose heart! Though our outward
humanity is in decay, yet day by day we are inwardly
renewed. Our troubles are slight and short-lived; and
their outcome an eternal glory which outweighs them far.
Meanwhile our eyes are fixed, not on the things that are
seen, but on the things that are unseen: for what is seen
passes away; but what is unseen is eternal. For we know
that if the earthly frame that houses us today should
be demolished, we possess a building which God has provided – a house not made by human hands, eternal, and
in heaven.   2 Corinthians 4.14, 16–18; 5.1 NEB

With all these witnesses to faith around us like a cloud, we
must throw off every encumbrance, every sin to which
we cling, and run with resolution the race for which we
are entered, our eyes fixed on Jesus, on whom faith
depends from start to finish: Jesus who, for the sake of the
joy that lay ahead of him, endured the cross, making light
of its disgrace, and has taken his seat at the right hand of
the throne of God.   Hebrews 12.1–2 NEB

Praise be to the God and Father of our Lord Jesus Christ,
who in his great mercy gave us new birth into a living hope
by the resurrection of Jesus Christ from the dead! The
inheritance to which we are born is one that nothing can

destroy or spoil or wither. It is kept for you in heaven, and you, because you put your faith in God, are under the protection of his power until salvation comes – the salvation which is even now in readiness and will be revealed at the end of time.

This is cause for great joy, even though now you smart for a little while, if need be, under trials of many kinds. Even gold passes through the assayer's fire, and more precious than perishable gold is faith which has stood the test. These trials come so that your faith may prove itself worthy of all praise, glory and honour when Jesus Christ is revealed.   1 Peter 1.3–7 NEB

. . . I heard a voice from heaven, saying, 'Write this: "Happy are the dead who die in the faith of Christ! Henceforth," says the Spirit, "they may rest from their labours; for they take with them the record of their deeds." '   Revelation 14.13 NEB

Then I saw a new heaven and a new earth, for the first heaven and the first earth had vanished, and there was no longer any sea. I saw the holy city, new Jerusalem, coming down out of heaven from God, made ready like a bride adorned for her husband. I heard a loud voice proclaiming from the throne: 'Now at last God has his dwelling among men! He will dwell among them and they shall be his people, and God himself will be with them. He will wipe every tear from their eyes; there shall be an end to death, and to mourning and crying and pain; for the old order has passed away!'

Then he who sat on the throne said, 'Behold! I am making all things new!' (And he said to me, 'Write this down; for these words are trustworthy and true. Indeed they are already fulfilled.') I am the Alpha and the Omega, the beginning and the end. A draught from the water-springs of life will be my free gift to the thirsty. All this is the victor's heritage; and I will be his God and he shall be my son.

Revelation 21.1–7 NEB

REFLECTION

The Bible: book of tears

The Bible tells us of people weeping for various reasons. It is a compendium of human emotions, and we are consoled by its inclusion of tearful people, reminding us that God in his compassion understands us when we grieve and seeks to comfort us.

In the Old Testament Abraham wept over the death of his wife Sarah. Esau wept when his father Isaac refused to bestow his blessing. The brothers Jacob and Esau wept in joyful embrace. Facing hardships in the wilderness, the Israelites cried in distress, claiming it would have been better to have died in Egypt's bondage. Naomi's daughters-in-law, Orpha and Ruth, wept as she bade them farewell. The Israelites mourned the death of Samuel. Job's face was red with crying, his eyes swollen and circled with shadows. The psalmist was worn out with grief, every night his pillow soaked with his tears, and David wept inconsolably over the death of his son Absalom.

In the New Testament, Matthew told of Herod's massacre of the infants, recalling Jeremiah's prophecy of the sound of bitter weeping in Ramah, and Rachel crying for her dead children, unable to be consoled. The woman who anointed Jesus with alabaster perfume stood over him weeping, his feet wet with her tears. Simon Peter, filled with remorse at his denial of Jesus, left the courtyard crying bitterly. Women wept for Jesus as he carried his cross to Calvary. Confronted with the death and burial of Jesus, Mary Magdalene shed tears in her grief. Jesus, who had said 'blessed are those who mourn', wept at the death of his friend Lazarus. The apostle Paul said we are to 'weep

with those who weep' and John, in the Book of Revelation,
had a vision of the Kingdom of Heaven in which he saw God
wiping away all mourners' tears, for then there would be no
more death, grief, crying or pain.

David M. Owen

PRAYERS

Through the scriptures

Heavenly Father, you have given us the scriptures
that through them we may have eternal life
by believing in your son:
Help us to receive your word into our hearts
that we find light for our way,
strength in our weakness,
and comfort in our distress.

New Every Morning

Word of consolation

Lord, thy word abideth,
And our footsteps guideth;
Who its truth believeth
Light and joy receiveth.

Word of mercy, giving
Succour to the living;
Word of life, supplying
Comfort to the dying.

Henry Williams Baker (1821–77)

Our thanks for the Bible

O God, we thank you . . . for the sacred scriptures;
for the comfort the Bible has brought to the sorrowful, for
guidance offered to the bewildered, for its gracious promises

to the uncertain, for its
strength given to the weak, and for its
progressive revelation of yourself.

Leslie D. Weatherhead (1893–1976)

Lord of all hopefulness

Lord God,
The scripture says you make all things new.
Make all things new this day.
Give us such hope in you
That we become optimistic about everyone and
    everything else.
Lord of all hopefulness, Lord of the future,
Lead us forward with a light step and a courageous heart;
To your honour and glory,
And for the sake of Jesus Christ,
Your Son, our Saviour.

Jamie Wallace

2

The concept of the soul

John Cole, an Anglican priest who worked in physiological psychology, wrote in *The Times* of Archbishop Robert Runcie's visit to a dying woman in a hospice. She was an artist and a potter, and before he left she promised to send him her last piece of pottery. It soon arrived – a representation of a fractured and empty shell, a lasting token of her faith. The broken, empty shell symbolized the condition of her body; the chick that had emerged from it, her soul, was released from its enclosure and liberated into the fuller life for which it was intended, and which it was not able to achieve within the shell.

Cole added:

> A fertilised egg, although it contains the living cell with all its hidden potential, shows to the naked eye no sign of the future chick. But with warmth and the passage of time the life within develops, expanding until it breaks out of the shell, which it leaves behind empty; then in a new form it goes forward into the greater life which is its destiny. So it seems the soul develops in the body, eventually separating from it to enter that life about which it knows so little, but for which it has been preparing and been prepared within the physical confines of the flesh.
>
> *The Times*, 16 June 1984

Because of its intangible nature it is difficult to define the human soul. The Bible regards it as the self, or the life of a person: not a separate entity from the body and capable of existing without it, rather that which gives life to the body. Man does not so much *have* a soul: he *is* a soul.

By and large the New Testament continues this belief, but now the soul, or 'psyche', is more personalized and important to a man's vital decision making. He may win the whole world, but lose his soul or self, and yet by self-sacrifice he can succeed in keeping it (Mark 8.34–47).

The soul's mystery is its glory, and our inability to define it satisfactorily is a testimony to its boundless freedom. Restricted in this life because of mental and bodily limitations, it yet soars at times to unimaginable heights of thought and faith. How much greater will be its scope when, in its new body in heaven, it finds perfect freedom!

My soul is me, your soul is you – indestructible, eternal, with a capacity to know and enjoy God for ever – and we may trust him to see us safely through death to life.

REFLECTIONS

More than our physical parts

Many people in our own society and others believe that we have souls that live on when we die. The word soul is important for it indicates that we are more than the sum of our individual physical parts. We can pray, recognise right and wrong, love and think creative thoughts. It is obvious that there is some relationship between our mental activity and the electrical and chemical processes that go on in the brain. Certain operations on the brain can change our character, drugs can alter our mood. But this does not mean that our mental activity will cease to function with the death of our brains. Some scientists have argued that mind is in fact prior to, and independent of the brain, which acts as a kind of focus or transmitter of mental activity. Though there is a correspondence between what goes on in the mind and what goes on in the brain, the former may be only temporally dependent on the latter. Whatever the truth of this matter, the Christian faith bases its belief in life everlasting not on anything inherently immortal about us, but upon God's revealed character as one who loves and wants us.

Richard Harries

The real me

So, what is the soul then? It must be the 'real me'. This certainly isn't the material of my body, because that's changing all the time. I have very few atoms left from among those that were there a few years ago. Eating and drinking, wear and tear, mean that they're continually being replaced. The real me is . . . not limited within the confines of my skin but, in some way, it must include also those significant relationships that do so much to constitute me as a person. It is beyond our present abilities to formulate these ideas more precisely, but it seems an intelligent and coherent hope that God will remember the pattern that is me and recreate it in a new environment of God's choosing, by a great act of final resurrection. Christian belief in a destiny beyond death has always centred on resurrection, not survival. Christ's Resurrection is the foretaste and guarantee, within history, of our resurrection, which awaits us beyond history.

John Polkinghorne

Immortal soul

We know instinctively that there is nothing in man's spirit to wear away. Our soul is not in our brain or heart. Strictly speaking a man's soul cannot be located. For a spirit has neither shape nor size. By it the whole body is informed with life.

When death comes the spirit departs. The immortal soul, in the old phrase 'shakes off this mortal coil'. The soul cannot corrupt or fade or die. It cannot dissolve into parts because it has no parts. It is not made of matter and is indestructible.

But is it not possible that the Creator will destroy the life He gave? The answer is that it would be a denial of God's wisdom if He were to blot out the life of a soul. For a soul by nature is immortal. God could not have made the soul of a man immortal if it were destined to be annihilated.

John Heenan (1905–75), late Archbishop of Westminster

The inviolate soul

Imagine a man whose only means of communicating with others is by playing a violin. If his violin is taken and smashed, he is still a violinist. He still loves music. His ability is not destroyed. No one can touch that. 'Fear not them that kill the body,' said Jesus, 'and after that have no more that they can do' (Luke 12.4). The soul is inviolate and goes on into another phase of being, picks up another instrument, which Paul called 'the spiritual body' (1 Cor. 15.44) and plays even more glorious music than the physical body and brain could express.

Death, disease, mental disharmony and emotional disturbance may affect the body, the brain and the senses which depend on it. But all these were only instruments which the soul used on this plane of being. The inviolate soul will not have suffered deprivation let alone annihilation. God has had access to the soul all the time.

To those whose loved ones are dead, or mentally ill, or physically worn out, or ravaged with disease, I would say 'Be of good cheer! The soul is inviolate. It dwells in the innermost sanctuary of the being. God keeps its key on His girdle and none may enter but He.'

Leslie D. Weatherhead (1893–1976)

Survival of the spirit

It is more likely in my particular cancer than in many others – and certainly than in other cases of terminal illness – for the body to become wasted and distorted almost beyond recognition, yet for the spirit, the inner man, the personality, to remain as it was before the illness began. If the spirit can survive such gross mutilation of its 'container', is it not reasonable to suppose it will survive physical death?

Dr James Casson, a testimony before his death

Like a baby in the womb

The soul, like a baby in the womb, appears to reach a stage of development when it is ready to leave behind the shelter of the body in which it has lived and grown, and emerge into the fuller life.

This cannot be shown to be true by rational argument nor by logical proof, but is the witness of many who tend the dying and of the dying themselves. Such witnesses and our own faith reveal to us that the ultimate is not death, itself imprisoned in the temporal, but life in God, the eternal, the alpha and omega, from whom the soul came and to whom it returns.

John Cole

God in the soul

The air is in the sunshine and the sunshine in the air. So likewise is God in the being of the soul; and whenever the soul's highest powers are turned inward with active love, they are united with God without means, in a simple knowledge of all truth, and in an essential feeling and tasting of all good.

Jan van Ruysbroeck (1293/4–1381)

Unshackle my soul

O Holy Spirit, unshackle my soul
from every dungeon which shuts it in,
and would shut thee out:
give it wings of the morning
and the jubilation of the freed
to fly to its home, its rest, its Lord.
Come, O Holy Spirit, come in thy blessed mercy
and set me free.

Eric Milner-White (1884–1963)

Kingdom of the soul

There comes a moment when man wearies of the things he has won; when he suspects with bewilderment and dismay that there is another purpose, some profound and eternal purpose in his being. It is then that he discovers that beyond the kingdom of the world there exists a kingdom of the soul.

A. J. Cronin (1896–1981)

The soul's march

Instead of saying that the soul of man goes marching on to God it would be truer to Christian belief to say that *God goes marching on and that because He does He wills that the souls of men, by His power shall march with Him.* In other words a doctrine of immortality must be built primarily upon the nature of God and His purpose. That purpose is big enough to include man. We know this because when God made himself fully known it was through a human life, the life of Jesus. It is in the rising of this Jesus from the dead that the promise and pledge of our immortality is to be found. Once we see this we can allow the vigorous, poetic language about the soul of man marching on to God. Man can march on to God because God marches with him.

Charles Duthie (1911–81)

Possessing my soul

They took away what should have been my eyes,
(But I remembered Milton's Paradise).
They took away what should have been my ears,
(Beethoven came and wiped away my tears).
They took away what should have been my tongue,
(But I had talked with God when I was young).
He would not let them take my soul –
Possessing that, I still possess the whole.

Helen Keller (1880–1968)

Hope of the soul

Hope is the struggle of the soul, breaking loose from what is perishable, and attesting her eternity.

Herman Melville (1819–91)

As at Tenebrae . . .

A hundred years ago, George Tyrrell, the Roman Catholic priest whose Modernist views finally led to his excommunication, wrote of the evening office of Tenebrae when all the candles are slowly extinguished except for the highest of all:

As at Tenebrae, one after another the lights are extinguished, till one alone – and that the highest of all – is left, so it is often with the soul and her guiding stars. In our early days there are many – parents, teachers, friends, books, authorities – but, as life goes on, one by one they fall and leave us in deepening darkness, with an increasing sense of the mystery and inexplicability of all things, till at last none but the figure of Christ stands out, luminous against the prevailing night.

That solitary figure stands at the heart of my own *cantus firmus*.

Michael Mayne (1929–2006)

PRAYERS

My soul, thy gift

The soul which thou has given me is pure.
Thou didst form it; thou didst breath it
into me; thou preservest it within me;
thou wilt take it from me, but will restore
it unto me hereafter . . . Blessed art thou,
source of eternal life.

A Jewish prayer

Prepare my soul

> O Thou Who hast prepared a place for my soul,
> Prepare my soul for that place:
> Prepare it with holiness,
> Prepare it with desire;
> And even while it sojourneth upon earth
> Let it dwell in heaven with Thee
> Beholding the beauty of Thy countenance,
> And the glory of Thy Saints,
> Now and forever.

Joseph Hall (1574–1656)

Go forth, Christian soul

Go forth upon thy journey from this world, O Christian
  soul,
in the peace of him in whom thou hast believed,
in the name of God the Father, who created thee,
in the name of Jesus Christ, who suffered for thee,
in the name of the Holy Spirit, who strengthened thee.
May angels and archangels, and all the armies of the
  heavenly host come to meet thee,
may all the saints of God welcome thee,
may thy portion this day be in gladness and peace, thy
  dwelling in Paradise.
Go forth upon thy journey, O Christian Soul.

Prayer for the dying, from the Roman Ritual

The souls of the faithful

May the souls of the faithful, through the mercy of God, rest
in peace.

An ancient collect at Compline

Touch my soul

O heavenly Father, touch and penetrate and shake and waken the inmost depth and centre of my soul, that all that is within me may cry and call to you. Strike the flinty rock of my heart that the water of eternal life may spring up in it. Oh break open the gates of the great deep in my soul, that your light may shine in upon me, that I may enter into your Kingdom of light and love, and in your light see light.

William Law (1686–1761)

At my soul's loosing

As you love me,
Let there be no mourning when I go,
Rather of your sweet courtesy
Rejoice with me
At my soul's loosing from captivity.

Author unknown

3

Death no stranger

Birth is common to us all, and so is death. We are born to live, hopefully into old age and in happiness through the years, but then we must depart this life. Death is the great leveller, for monarchs and peasants, saints and sinners all die.

Nor during our lifetime here can any of us avoid meeting death in others, or the personal and painful experience of bereavement. We lose loved ones and colleagues, and the media daily records the passing of public figures and a host of names unknown to us. Each week in my hospital chaplaincy work I would visit the maternity ward and discover the joys of new life, but almost as frequently I would be at the crematorium or cemetery laying to rest the body of one whose life had been completed. Life and death are inextricably linked, and this is not at all a morbid thought; on the contrary, it is exciting, for it means our living is an adventure and responsibility, and our death a commitment and fulfilment.

We rightly put much thought and energy into living as fully as we can. While we are not expected to go around every day thinking about death, it would be irresponsible of us to be so preoccupied with the here and now that we never think of death at all.

We do need to think about it in order to prepare ourselves for it, and we should learn to speak of it with greater ease. It is a perfectly natural occurrence, just like birth, but while we were not conscious of life in the womb, and could do nothing to prepare for our release into the outside world, we can prepare for our own death. Perhaps the actual moment of our dying will be an unconscious one, or it might be the most conscious and exhilarating we have ever known. In the meantime we can prepare ourselves for this momentous occasion – in fact, the whole of life is a time of preparation and we should never be so busy with worldly pursuits that death loses its place in our thinking.

We prepare for dying and death by honestly and constantly facing the truth about our mortality. It is said that Philip of Macedonia, the great warrior king of the fourth century BC, appointed a courtier to whisper to him every day, 'Philip, remember thou too art mortal.' He was wise enough to know he needed to heed the warning, lest he should think himself a god.

We too are mortal, in common with every human being of every age, without exception. But how sad if our preparation was merely to see us through to the end and then oblivion! We believe otherwise, for that would be a terrible travesty and a total discouragement, indeed, a mockery of our aspirations. Mortal we are in body, but immortal in soul. Add to that agelong belief, which is not specifically Christian, the teaching of the New Testament of Christ's resurrection and ours, and we can face the end of our earthly life and its beyond with confidence and joy.

REFLECTIONS

But life is immortal

Men are indeed brothers, of each other and of the humblest form used by the one life. They should live as such; they should regard death from this point of view. Life never dies; only the forms of life. The opposite of death is not life but birth. All that is born dies, but life is immortal . . .

Christmas Humphreys (1901–83), an English Buddhist

Death does matter

It is hard to have patience with people who say 'There is no death' or 'Death doesn't matter'. There is death. And whatever is matters. And whatever happens has consequences, and it and they are irrevocable and irreversible. You might as well say that birth doesn't matter. I look up at the night sky. Is anything more certain than that in all those vast times and spaces, if I were allowed to search them, I should nowhere find her face, her voice, her touch? She died. She is dead. Is the word so difficult to learn?

C. S. Lewis (1898–1963)

Do not gloat over the death of anyone;
Remember we all must die.

Ecclesiasticus 8.7 REB

Involved in mankind

Any man's death diminishes me, because I am involved in mankind; and therefore never send to know for whom the bell tolls; it tolls for thee.

John Donne (1571–1631)

Death in life

In the midst of life we are in death.

Book of Common Prayer (1662)

Treated all alike

Death, the only immortal who treats us all alike, whose pity and whose peace and whose refuge are for all – the soiled and the pure, the rich and the poor, the loved and the unloved.

Mark Twain (1835–1910), his last words

PRAYERS

Help for those who suffer

O heavenly Father,
we pray for those suffering from diseases
for which there is at present no cure.
Give them the victory of trust and hope,
that they may never lose their faith
in your loving purpose.
Grant your wisdom to all
who are working to discover the causes
of disease,
and the realisation that through you
all things are possible.
We ask this in the name of him
who went about doing good
and healing all manner of sickness,
even your Son, Jesus Christ, our Lord.

George Appleton (1902–93)

While I'm here

Lord, help me to live, knowing that I will depart one day. So let me, while I enjoy life's blessings, have before me the eternal view, and not get over-fond of material things.

David M. Owen

Death as part of life

Lord, it bothers me to hear so much talk about death. Death is a constant news item, and I keep hearing of the passing of people I have known. In my despondent moments, Lord, I am inclined to think there's more death than life.

Forgive me for not seeing clearly that death is part of life, a rhythm as important as day and night, and that our comings and goings are in your hands, perfectly controlled and brought to fruition.

Help me to accept what is really your purpose for us all, and to meet all such happenings with a quiet faith.

David M. Owen

Simply for love of you

Glorious God, give me grace to amend my life, and to have an eye to my end without begrudging death, which to those who die in you, good Lord, is the gate of a wealthy life.

Give me, good Lord, a longing to be with you, not to avoid the calamities of this world, nor so much to attain the joys of heaven, as simply for love of you.

Thomas More (1478–1535)

4

Fear and faith

Most of us have fears – fears of failure, loneliness, war, dangers facing our loved ones, and perhaps most of all, fears of the process of dying and of the 'Unknown Beyond'. How will we cope with pain and physical deterioration? Will we lose our mental faculties? Will death be oblivion cutting us off for ever from our cherished relationships? Or, if there is a judgement of us, how will we measure up? And if there is a punishment for our sins, how will we bear it?

In his 'Hymn to God the Father', John Donne admits his fears about meeting death and of the consequences of his sins, but his hope rests in God's pardon and peace:

> I have a sin of fear that when I have spun
> My last thread, I shall perish on the shore;
> Swear by thy self that at my death, thy Sun
> Shall shine as it shines now, and heretofore;
> And having done that, thou hast done,
>   I have no more.

Fear in itself is not a sin. There are healthy fears that prevent recklessness and increase caution. A mountaineer or round-the-world yachtsman who had no fear of the elements would make a dangerous companion. Fear reminds us of life's vulnerability and fragility, and it is a healthy fear that produces fortitude and heroism. Our mistake is to let fear become fearfulness, so that we lose our composure and give way to despair. Such a condition is a denial of faith in God's providence.

I am sure God understands if we have fears in the face of dying and death, and does not condemn us for them. Let us confess them and seek reassurance from the Scriptures, through prayer and with the help of wise counsellors.

There is, though, a fear that must remain – the fear of God; not that of terror but of awe in the face of his mysteries that await us. When the psalmist said, 'The fear of the LORD is the beginning of wisdom' (Psalm 111.10 NEB), he did not mean that we are to be frightened of him and so dread his presence, rather that we have an awed regard for his holiness and a proper concern for those sins which offend and cause him pain. It is an attitude of reverence before him and a call to righteous living.

It is to our comfort and encouragement that Jesus feared his coming death. Shortly after he had told his disciples not to let their hearts be troubled, his own heart was in distress. He dreaded the cup of suffering leading to death, and prayed for its removal, and that brings him wonderfully close to us in any fears that we might have. His eventual acceptance of the cup lay in his deep trust in God his Father, to whom at the end he committed his spirit.

REFLECTIONS

Fear itself
The only thing we have to fear is fear itself.

Franklin D. Roosevelt (1882–1945)

Fear so great
Our fear of death is so great that the whole of life is but keeping away the thought of it.

The Times

Fearing the pain
It is not death or pain that is to be dreaded, but the fear of pain or death.

Epictetus (*c.* 55–*c.* 135)

If you worry

Bel Mooney in The Times *responds to a letter from a woman afraid of her impending death:*

Well, old Faustus had plenty to worry about but you do not – other than the *timor mortis conturbat me* (fear of death worries me) which is the refrain of anonymous medieval lyrics. If you worry about not being able to control the uncontrollable, if you allow your fears to dominate your nights, you will feel tired and stressed, and nothing is more ageing than that. Please don't collude in this shortening of your life by worrying about its end . . .

. . . I don't know what others do, but my way of coping is to reflect calmly on death every single day. Around my house I have little Mexican skulls for the Day of the Dead, and other jovial reminders of my own mortality. They tell me to seize the time. They remind me, when I pinch the skin on my arm and see how wrinkly it is, not to see the sight as a grim warning but to feel the hard little pinch as proof that I am alive: a feeling, sentient being with so much life in me yet. By meditating on, and accepting the prospect of your own death, you can fling yourself more actively into a present of celebration . . .

The land is bright

Say not – the struggle nought availeth,
The labour and the wounds are vain,
The enemy faints not, nor faileth –
And as things have been, they remain!

For while the tired waves, vainly breaking,
Seem here no painful inch to gain,
Far back, through creeks and inlets making,
Comes silent – flooding in – the main.

And not by eastern windows only,
When daylight comes, comes in the light;

In front, the sun climbs slow – how slowly!
But westward – look! The land is bright.

Arthur Hugh Clough (1819–61)

You have rescued me from death
and my feet from stumbling,
to walk in the presence of God,
in the light of life.

Psalm 56.13 REB

Do not be afraid. I am the first and the last, and I am the living one; for I was dead and now I am alive for evermore, and I hold the keys of Death and Death's domain.

Revelation 1.18 NEB

I shall love death as well

It is the same life that shoots in joy through the dust of the earth in numberless blades of grass, and breaks into tumultuous waves of leaves and flowers. It is the same life that is rocked in the ocean-cradle of birth and of death, in ebb and flow. Because I love this life, I know I shall love death as well.

Rabindranath Tagore (1861–1941)

Jesus in the Garden

When we turn to the most perfect life of all, we do not find that it was lived without fear. Indeed, we find recorded by a doctor a symptom of fear which shows a depth of anguish rarely realized in the lives of men. 'His sweat became, as it were, great drops of blood falling down upon the ground.' This is a symptom of extreme anguish of mind which is rarely witnessed. The courage of Jesus is not that negative quality based on literal fearlessness. Surely it is true to say that the measure of his courage was the measure of his overcome fear. One would have been impossible without the other. And when the shadow of the cross loomed up so close to him that even he cried, 'if it be possible to let this cup pass,' he proceeded to take such an attitude to calamity that he wrung from the situation the courage only commensurate with the fear which that situation was capable of producing.

I believe that he can bring men to the point when they realize that there is no situation capable of defeating the human spirit; when the measure of the most terrible calamity the mind can imagine becomes the measure of courage which can be made out of the situation in order to overcome it.

Leslie D. Weatherhead (1893–1976)

To live and die

Teach me to live, that I may dread
The grave as little as my bed;
Teach me to die, that so I may
Rise glorious at the aweful day.

Thomas Ken (1637–1711)

Death – my fears

What do I *fear* about death?

(1) Being unable to cope with it when it comes.

(2) Being cut off 'prematurely', before I am ready. I have a nasty feeling that I shall be yanked unceremoniously out of this life, with all sorts of loose ends and unfinished business.

(3) What is probably worse: a dreary, drawn-out process of dying, with the family visiting and everyone getting depressed; with me getting weaker, like an old banger running out of power going up a steep hill.

(4) Being unable to receive the Sacraments, or at least make a proper act of repentance and spiritual Communion.

(5) The distress of those I love, and my distress with and for them.

(6) Dying messily and painfully, over a steering wheel or collapsed in a lavatory.

(7) On the other hand, having *too much time*, so that I might lose my nerve and give way to cowardice or whining (verbally or inwardly), sinking into self-pity, etc.

(8) Dying unconscious or in my sleep. On the other hand, having experienced acute physical pain, I do not relish that either.

So, however I look at it, I must reconcile myself to the fact that my death will not be arranged perfectly and I must be ready to 'die well' whatever the circumstances. In fact, I want to *resign* myself to whatever death I die; or, rather, to God in my dying.

Graham Smith

PRAYERS

Made for life

Heavenly Father, you have not made us
for darkness and death, but for life
with you for ever.
Without you we have nothing to hope for;
with you we have nothing to fear.
Speak to us now your words of eternal life.
Lift us from anxiety and guilt
to the light and peace of your presence,
and set the glory of your love before us;
through Jesus Christ our Lord. Amen.

Pocket Words of Comfort

Watch, O Lord

Watch thou, O Lord, with those who wake,
or watch, or weep tonight, and give thine
angels charge over those who sleep. Tend
thy sick ones, O Lord Christ; rest thy

weary ones; bless thy dying ones; soothe
thy suffering ones; pity thine afflicted
ones; shield thy joyous ones, and all for
thy love's sake.

St Augustine of Hippo (353–430)

In whom is all our hope

Eternal God, in whom is all our hope
in life, in death, and to all eternity;
grant that, rejoicing in the eternal life
which is ours in Christ,
we may face whatever the future holds in store for us calm
    and unafraid,
always confident that neither death nor life
can part us from your love in Jesus Christ our Lord.

James M. Todd

Lighten our darkness

Lighten our darkness,
Lord, we pray; and in your mercy defend us
from all dangers and perils of this night;
for the love of your only Son,
our Lord Jesus Christ. Amen.

Alternative Service Book (1980)

For those who fear

Lord of consolation, we commend to you those who live in constant fear – afraid of the hurt that others may inflict on them, afraid of illness, accident, worried about those they love, afraid of dying and of death and beyond. Comfort and grant them confidence in their despair, a trust in committing all to your caring love, and a greater happiness in the days to come.

David M. Owen

Lord, I'm afraid

Lord, I am afraid of dying. I think I love you and want to be with you but the thought of going from this world into the unknown is terrifying. I begin to wonder if you exist. O Lord, help me, give me some reassurance that you will be with me unto the end of the world and beyond it into the next.

Michael Hollings and Etta Gullick

5

This life in preparation

———◆———

The Anglican Series 3 Litany bids us pray, 'From violence, murder, and *dying unprepared*, Good Lord, deliver us.'

To die, prepared or unprepared, implies a period of life, long or short, in which we accept or reject that responsibility. We therefore see this world as a training ground for our meeting with death and the new life that awaits us beyond death. Death itself is a test of life's fundamental questions about belief and behaviour. How truly do I believe in God? What does my life here add up to? How well have I lived, and what have I done to make this world a better place?

If we are to find satisfactory answers to such deep ponderings we need to wrestle throughout life with the mystery and challenge of death. The Swiss psychiatrist Carl Jung saw death as a goal towards which we strive, so that to shrink from it is unhealthy for us. He argued that as we get older death ought to occupy our minds much more, and that if we thought more of death we should make more of life.

We confidently assert that our life in this world, and the world itself, are God's most basic and precious gifts to us, which he expects us to use wisely and well. When the psalmist said, 'The earth is the Lord's and all that is in it, the world and those who dwell therein' (Psalm 24.1 NEB), he was expressing a positive faith that all he saw belonged to the Lord. His view was world affirming and not world denying, and this is important in our understanding of life as a preparation for death and the future life. Here we live to die, not in any morbid or negative sense, not as those who despise this world, and not as some eager religious martyrs who have too readily yielded up their life. Death will come to each of us in time; meanwhile let us live each day to the full, knowing that each day and each deed are important to what we are now and to what we shall be.

REFLECTIONS

The moment of ecstasy

This life is a period of training, a time of preparation, during which we learn the art of loving God and our neighbour, the heart of the Gospel message, sometimes succeeding, sometimes failing.

Death is the way which leads us to the vision of God, the moment when we shall see Him as He really is, and find our total fulfilment in love's final choice.

The ultimate union with that which is most lovable, union with God, is the moment of ecstasy, the unending 'now' of complete happiness. That vision will draw from us the response of surprise, wonder and joy which will be forever our prayer of praise. We are made for that.

Basil Hume (1923–99)

One day I shall die

We live in a rapidly changing world. Nothing is certain. One thing is: we all face death.

It is a sombre thought. We find all sorts of ways of forgetting about it. We use expressions which empty it of finality and threat. We talk about 'going to the other side' or 'passing away'. Yet it is the Christian instinct to be brave and to face the meaning of death fairly and squarely. We face it because it is inescapable, one of life's harsh realities. Whenever a member of the family, or a colleague, dies we are reminded very vividly that it is the one thing that will happen to each one of us. Dying can be a very lonesome experience, for nothing can be more isolating than pain.

One day I shall die. Thinking about that is good for me. It helps me to look at the way I am living. It enables me to get a better perspective. I know that I shall not remain forever in this world. I must ask important questions: 'Am I making the best of my life? Am I living in such a way that I try always to follow my conscience? Are my motives in life right? What do I really want? What am I really seeking?' Those are very simple and fundamental questions, and ones that we have to ask ourselves.

That is a sobering thought. While such thoughts have their value, it would be quite wrong to leave it like that. The Christian faces death realistically, but also knows that death is a gateway, a new beginning, a fulfilment of human life.

I fail to understand how anyone can go through life and think there is nothing after death. That is a totally inhuman thought. Now life for the majority is not easy. There are periods of joy and happiness of course; there are times when things go smoothly and happily; yet there are a great number of times when it is a burden. Life is punctuated now with joys, now with sorrows. Within us is the desire to live; we want to go on. There is an urge to go on living fully and totally. We long to enjoy deep down the peace, the joy and happiness which constantly elude us. We cannot grasp them now nor keep them.

It is for that deep joy and happiness that we were made. One day it will be ours. If it were not going to be ours our lives would certainly end in frustration and be unfulfilled. That is not only a terrible thing to contemplate, but it is to my way of thinking unreasonable.

We are men and women moving through life like pilgrims headed towards our final destination. It is healthy to look forward to that destination when we shall find total fulfilment. That fulfilment must consist in an experience of love because love is the highest of all human experience. To love totally, to be loved completely. It is in union with that which is most lovable that we become fully ourselves.

Do not be fearful of death. Welcome it when it comes. It is now a holy thing, made so by him who died that we might live.

Basil Hume (1923–99)

If a man would live well

If a man would live well, let him fetch his last day to him, and make it always his company-keeper.

John Bunyan (1628–88)

Take care

Take care of your life; and the Lord will take care of your death.

George Whitefield (1714–70)

Unto our destiny

God does not just cast us off as discarded broken pots, thrown on to the rubbish heap of the universe when we die. Our belief in a destiny beyond our death rests in the loving faithfulness of the eternal God.

John Polkinghorne

Life – a dying

All of life is itself a dying. My existence today is built upon the death of my yesterday; and my today will perish so that my tomorrow may come.

Norman Pittenger (1905–97)

Part of a larger pattern

I have an absolute conviction, without any qualification what-soever, that this life that we live in time and in space for three-score years and ten is not the whole story; that it is only part of a larger story. Therefore, death cannot be for others, or for one's self, an end, any more than birth is a beginning. Death is part of a larger pattern; it fits into a larger, eternal scale, not simply a time scale . . . I think of my own death as something which will transform my way of living into another mode of living rather than as an end; and one thinks of others whom one has loved and who have died as equally participating in that other existence, in that larger dimension. To me this is completely satisfying. I don't want to know any more than this.

Malcolm Muggeridge (1903–90)

For life and death are one

> You would know the secret of death,
> But how shall you find it unless you seek it in the
>   heart of life?
> The Owl, whose night-bound eyes are blind
>   unto the day, cannot unveil the mystery of
>   light,
> If you would indeed behold the spirit of death,
>   open up your heart wide into the body of life,
> For life and death are one, even as the river and
>   the sea are one.

Kahlil Gibran (1883–1931)

The lesson from nature

In nature death is not the end of life, but a means by which life is fulfilled and enriched; it has a positive as well as a negative element. Those who view death as the 'endless endingness of everything, all that going down into the grave' have, as yet, failed to see that this gloom is dispelled by the joy of endless beginnings, by all that life emerging from the bud, the shell and the womb.

The decay of autumn is necessary for the coming of spring, the leaf falls that the bud may grow, shell and womb that have sheltered the growing life perish, but the life goes on to fulfil its destiny. The widow mourning her husband finds comfort in seeing his life and hers continuing in their children and grandchildren.

John Cole

PRAYERS

To live every day

Who can tell what a day may bring forth? Cause me therefore, gracious God, to live every day as if it were to be my last, for I know not but that it may be such. Cause me to live now as I shall wish I had done when I come to die. O grant that I may not die with any guilt on my conscience, or any known sin unrepented of, but that I may be found in Christ, who is my only Saviour and Redeemer.

Thomas à Kempis (1380–1471)

Thanks for life

I thank Thee, God, that I have lived
In this great world and known its many joys;
The song of birds, the strong, sweet scent of hay
And cooling breezes in the secret dusk,
The flaming sunsets at the close of day,
Hills, and the lonely, heather-covered moors,
Music at night, and moonlight on the sea,
The beat of waves upon the rocky shore
And wild, white spray, flung high in ecstasy;
The faithful eyes of dogs, and treasured books.
The love of kin and fellowship of friends,
And all that makes life dear and beautiful.
I thank Thee, too, that there has come to me
A little sorrow and, sometimes, defeat,
A little heartache and the loneliness
That comes with parting, and the word,
   'Goodbye',
Dawn breaking after dreary hours of pain,
When I discovered that night's gloom must yield
And morning light break through to me again.
Because of these and other blessings poured
Unasked upon my wondering head,

Because I know that there is yet to come
An even richer and more glorious life,
And most of all, because Thine only Son
Once sacrificed life's loveliness for me –
I thank Thee, God, that I have lived.

Elizabeth, Countess of Craven (1750–1828)

Lord, you are life

Jesus, Lord, you are life
Always and everywhere;
In creation you are life,
In the world you are life,
In the Church you are life.
When death shall still our mortal bodies,
You, Lord, will be our life eternally.

David M. Owen

Work and life

God give me work
Till my life shall end,
And life
Till my work is done.

Charles F. Shepherd

And our work is done

O Lord, support us all the day long of this troublous life, until
the shadows lengthen, and the evening comes, and the busy world
is hushed, the fever of life is over, and our work is done. Then,
Lord, in your mercy, grant us safe lodging, a holy rest, and peace
at the last; through Jesus Christ our Lord.

John Henry Newman (1801–90)

6

Too soon to die

The death of a child is particularly harrowing. Youngsters are expected to enjoy life over many years within a family and among friends, to engage in a worthwhile job, and in many cases to become parents and grandparents themselves. While it may be true that one young life can contribute more in a short time than that of an elderly person over a longer period, nevertheless we'd all agree that a young death is a tragic deprivation – in a way, the theft of a priceless treasure intended for us all. But it does happen, as well we know through the daily media. A life full of promise is ended due to illness, accident, alcohol or drug abuse, or from desperate depression, and the emotional pain suffered by loved ones bearing the loss is excruciating.

Over recent months in the UK we have all heard of the several young people brutally killed with guns and knives, and the consequent grief of their parents, families and friends.

In many cases, parents grieving for a lost child may suffer an added strain in their relationship. They may be unable to talk to one another about their feelings at the very time they need to be closer, and sometimes the result is a complete separation. Everything should be done to avoid this happening, to take time to understand each other's emotions (women and men do vary in their ability to do this), and to be strong for each other. The cultivation of happy memories, allowing recollections of their child's life to surround their home and their hearts, will help to bring comfort and healing. I heard of one family who continued to celebrate their deceased child's birthday by inviting other youngsters to a party. This must have been difficult, but it was one way of keeping their happy memories before them.

And, of course, children themselves suffer bereavement through the loss of a parent or a brother or sister, a close relative or friend, and grown-ups need to be very sensitive and caring. Even their parents' separation can be a kind of family death, leaving children bereft and with behavioural difficulties. The Child Bereavement Trust provides useful information about such problems. Children's capacity to cope with difficult emotions increases with age and maturity. There may be an apparent lack of sadness, but this does not mean they are not grieving. There are behavioural signs that need to be seen and understood by parents, teachers and all who are involved in the child's upbringing.

Young children may bed-wet, suffer tummy upsets, nightmares or lack of concentration, may exhibit excessively attention-seeking behaviour and become clingy. Older children often show variations from their normal behaviour, including depression, rudeness, not wanting to attend school, and general under-achievement. Bereaved adolescents may regress to a younger, more dependent stage in their development. In their search for love and affection they may develop premature new sexual relationships. Their emotions may be suppressed, resulting in a display of apparent indifference or lack of feelings.

Young people may turn to truancy or petty delinquency as a protest against the upheaval within their family. Some will withdraw to grieve in the solitude of their own room. Self-destructive behaviour such as excessive drinking or drug taking may be their way of coping with grief. By confronting death they try to overcome their fears, and demonstrate control over their own mortality. Some young people assume the parental role, taking on heavy responsibilities, causing them to mature rapidly, and denying themselves the opportunity or permission to grieve.

The Child Bereavement Trust encourages grieving children, young people and families to write or email their sad experiences: it helps them to do so, and can be beneficial to others who are grieving by lessening their sense of isolation.

Bob wrote of the death of two-year-old Simon: 'How is it possible to recover from that? It felt like a bid for survival.' Jim and Elspeth wrote of the 'perfect family' they had enjoyed until four-month-old Lindsay died in her pram, a victim of cot death. Sixteen-year-old Nichola experienced the deaths of both her brother and sister from cystic fibrosis just six weeks apart. Daniel looked on his brother Jason, nine years his senior, as one would look up to a film star or sporting legend. Then came his shattering blow – Jason took his own life. Other couples have written of the terrible dilemma of having to terminate a pregnancy on medical advice, or of the shocking disappointment of a stillborn child. Somewhere, every day, someone is suffering these terrible agonies.

It is little wonder that a life cut short evokes the most soul-searching questions. Why are children denied their years of happiness and fulfilment? If God has a plan for each new life, why is it disrupted before reaching, at least, a measure of maturity?

We gain nothing and lose much by blaming God. Premature death is not his will. Jesus' love for children (Matthew 19.13–15) and his high estimate of their value (Matthew 18.1–7) tell the true story – the kingdom of heaven is theirs, and they are a shining example of humility to all.

The fact that children die, or that someone's life is terminated in the middle years when others go on to old age, will always seem unfair. And talk about the quality of life being more important than the quantity of years, although deeply true, is not guaranteed to bring immediate comfort to distraught parents, to a young widow bereft of her equally young husband, or to her children dispossessed of a father.

Nor, indeed, does everyone at this time of intense grief find the reassurance of a future life in which the imbalance is redressed. (Close company and respectful silence will probably be of more help.) But such reasoning is not unsound, for if God is a loving Father, as Jesus asserted, then should we not trust him to provide amply for those whom we have loved and lost too soon? Many have found comfort in the thought that our departed children are safe in the love of Jesus, and are led by him to their fulfilment. So too the others who died in middle life with so much left undone. In my reading of letters and emails from grieving parents I find that many assert this hope – indeed belief – in a future life after death for their deceased young ones. And it is more than wishful thinking designed to relieve the pain of grief, rather it expresses the deepest and most innate of human aspirations, a God-given support to help us face the sorrows of our earthly journey. The very character of God is judged on this matter, as is the life and teaching of Jesus.

In our reading of the Gospels we find that Jesus too encountered the sad experience of a child's terminal illness and parental distress. Jairus' cry at Capernaum said it all: 'My little daughter is at death's door, I beg you to come and lay your hands on her to cure her and save her life' (Mark 5.23 NEB). And at Nain, a young man, but still a mother's child, had died leaving her grief-stricken. The story is told in Luke 7.11–15, and it reveals a double tragedy. The woman had already suffered the loss of her husband, but with an only son as breadwinner she would have coped. Now she faced severe hardship. Luke's account of the funeral occasion reveals the deep compassion of Jesus, for when he saw the widow his heart went out to her. The meaning of that phrase here is that he was moved to the depths of his being, and it was an emotion Jesus showed in other situations.

To this day we believe Jesus shows that deep concern for both sick and dying children and their sorrowing parents as he did at Nain. The sorrow of this occasion in Nain was turned to joy, for this was one of Jesus' miracles when he raised the dead to life. In Luke 7.15 we find a lovely touch of tenderness, for as the dead man sat up and spoke we read, 'Jesus gave him back to his mother' (NEB).

While that miracle does not become literally true, for parents and children are physically separated at death, it is true in a spiritual sense and in terms of our faith. The child whose body has been destroyed by disease and death is now alive and secure in Jesus, who is the resurrection and the life. It is this belief and hope that is entrusted to sorrowing parents – a child secure in the love of Christ, in whom one day there will be a reunion.

REFLECTIONS

Sarah, aged seven

In the days shortly before her death, she would lie curled up in a chair, half-dozing, half-watching us as we lived out our lives around her. Smiling, she would say, 'I'm so happy, I feel I've got arms tight around me.' Her death was the most exciting moment of my life. Deep in the almost overwhelming pain and grief of her going I was still conscious of a great joy and triumph; joy that she had not been destroyed by her suffering, that she was still confident and reassured; joy that we were able to hand her back into and onto the greatest Love of all; joy that this was not really the end. I felt a very real sense of a new birth – more painful but as exciting as her first one seven years earlier. There was an inexplicable but unshakable knowledge that all was indeed well.

Jane Davies

Empty places

The tractor still sits on the shelf in the store,
The overalls rest in a box.
No cowboy boots tossed on the floor by the bed
While the cowboy 'rides horse' in his socks.

No sleepy-soft smiles as I nurse him to sleep,
After reading just one story more.
Vroom-vrooms and putt-putts aren't heard in the house
No little boy plays on the floor.

No hammer and nails in a two-year-old's hands,
As he struggles to build like his dad.
No smashed thumb, 'please rocky me, Mommy,' he sobs,
No spankings – he'll never be bad.

Two impish eyes full of mischief and glee,
Two dirt-smudged small cheeks I can't kiss,
Two little-boy arms giving back my quick hug,
These are some of the blessings we miss.

No boyish voice begging to go out with his dad,
Out fishing or hunting for deer,
No tousled blonde crew-cut asleep in his bed,
Drawing forth from my heart a love-tear.

Our new family picture is missing someone,
And so is our home-life it seems,
Yet a small boy goes galloping all 'round the room,
And he lives in my secret heart-dreams.

The tractor still waits on the shelf in the store,
His little lamb silently sleeps.
An empty place echoes a little boy's name
In the memories my dreaming heart keeps.

Arlene Stamy

Lament

*Similarly, Marjorie Pizer writes this lament for Glen who was killed
in a motorbike accident at the age of 19.*

The splendid youth is dead and is no more
And who shall comfort those who are left?

Who shall comfort the mother who has lost her son?
Who shall comfort the sisters who have lost a brother?
Who shall comfort the friends who have lost a friend?
And who shall comfort the father?
There is no comfort for those who are grieving,
For faith is not enough
To assuage the tearing wound of sudden death.
O let me not drown in the flood of grief
For all young men who died before their time,
And for this one, so newly dead.
O let me catch the raft of life again
And not be swept away
Into the darkest depths of grief and loss.

Marjorie Pizer

For myself, for my child

Just as surely as my child
Walked towards eternal life,
I too must walk towards my own light,
Finding a way through this
Tunnel of darkness,
To the brightness of a new day.

And in my own time,
Learn to live again
With laughter, love and joy –
For myself, for my child,
For those still in need.

So just for this moment,
Just for this day,
I set my hope
Upon tomorrow.

Author unknown

Too soon

This was a life
that had hardly begun
no time to find
your place in the sun
no time to do
all you could have done
but we loved you enough for a lifetime.

No time to enjoy
the world and its wealth
no time to take life
down off the shelf
no time to sing
the song of yourself
though you had enough love for a lifetime.

Those who live long
endure sadness and tears
but you'll never suffer
the sorrowing years:
no betrayal, no anger,
no hatred, no fears,
just love – only love – in your lifetime.

Mary Yarnell

When a drug addict dies

*Eric Blakeborough, MBE is Pastor Emeritus of the John Bunyan
Baptist Church, Kingston-upon-Thames, and Chairperson of the
Kaleidoscope Project which he founded in 1968. His book* No
Quick Fix *(1986) is an inspiring account of one church which
has taken seriously the practical application of the gospel and has
served Christ adventurously by developing a unique ministry to
the young homeless and among drug addicts. The project has*

gained recognition from governments and experts in social and community work.

When asked what is the attitude of Kaleidoscope when one of its drug addicts dies, Eric Blakeborough wrote this moving account.

When a drug addict dies there is sometimes a sense of inevitability. There is even a hope that this will act as a warning to others. But for the parents, their grief is heightened by a feeling of failure, guilt and anger. For some it seems best to get the funeral over as quickly as possible. In many cases, where the addict is estranged from parents, the Local Authority pays for a contract cremation with perhaps only a social worker, the duty clergyman and one or two mourners present. What is there to say?

At Kaleidoscope we recognize that drug users are a community, even if the 'drug scene' is classified as a 'sub group' by social commentators. The death of one of the people associated with Kaleidoscope, even if they are not in treatment, affects us all. There needs to be an occasion for expressing our sense of loss and grief. There may be an acute sense of guilt for some in our clients' community, and there may be a partner or a group of special friends who are heartbroken. Most of our clients are estranged from parents, but at this time many relations want to be included in our acts of remembrance, or they may want some personal contact.

The question prompted by the death of a drug addict is, what value do we attach to the life of the person who has died? If the funeral is an event to be got over as quickly and quietly as possible it can appear that the person who has died has been of little or no value. However others may judge them, we truly believe events and decisions which shape a person's lifestyle are complex beyond human understanding and are never that person's responsibility only. Christian theology does not support the notion that there are good people and bad people, 'all have sinned and come short of the glory of God'. The good news is that we are never beyond the love and redemptive power of God. The funeral rites must reflect this truth.

As Kaleidoscope is attached to a church it is usually appropriate that the funeral takes place in the church. This enables everyone who daily attends Kaleidoscope to come to the service, and a large number of our clients do usually attend. It is important that the style of the service reflects the experience of those who are present and that the words, music and actions relate to the person being remembered. At the same time, the service needs to give explicit expression to the religious feelings which are common, if dormant, in most people. Most people recognize that love is the highest virtue and are able to ascribe the power of redemptive love to God. Although only Christian believers are likely to have any understanding of salvation through the death and resurrection of Jesus, most people recognize that any credal statement means that the minister officiating at the funeral has confidence that in commending the dead person to the mercy of God there is hope of eternal life.

There is no doubt that people coming to Kaleidoscope find this ministry helpful. People look at the name in our Book of Remembrance. They recall the point of similarity with their own lives and they recognize that in honouring their companions who have died, we hold everyone in our community as precious. The reverence we show to each other, and the embraces which are shared, give us a reason for living now as well as pointing to a hope of life hereafter.

In God's completion

> That nothing walks with aimless feet;
> That not one life shall be destroy'd,
> Or cast as rubbish to the void,
> When God hath made the pile complete.

> Alfred, Lord Tennyson (1809–92)

The widow of Nain

A husband's death – what more can woman bear?
No emptiness compares, no loss nor pain,
One grievous hurt that lingers through the years.
Yet, in my one dear son that hurt was eased,
And he provided for my daily needs.
I was so proud of him, and hoped for him,
And lived because of him.
But cruel death, remorseless in its choice,
Came yet again to take away my son –
My son, my only son.
In lifeless flesh my pride and hope and life lay dead;
And still would be but for the Man of Nazareth.

I'll not forget the wailing cries that funeral day –
Well-meaning friends displaying grief in wilful tears.
But greater is the memory of this Man
Whose heart was moved to sorrow at my sorrow.
Urging me to 'cry not', he touched the coffin
And impelled my son –
'Young man, arise!'
And instantly he lived and talked,
And he was mine again – restored.

Dear Nain, what foretaste were you of that awful day
When, dead, they bore the body of this Man unto its rest,
And women wept,
His mother too – I understood her pain!
And you gave promise of that glorious day
When God's great prophet, sent to save us,
Did not dwell in death, but rose to walk and talk again,
No more to die.
All this you saw that day,
To give the world a glimpse of him –
The Resurrection and the Life.

David M. Owen
Based on Luke 7.11–17

Further stages of growth

For those who die young or tragically death is far from being a friend . . . it raises also the question of the possibility of further stages of growth after this life. So many die with lives cut short. Too many die after a lifetime of frustration and lack of fulfilment. If death is to be a friend of all there must be not only the possibility of life beyond it but a life in which all that has been stunted or nipped in the bud is enabled to grow.

Richard Harries

The unfinisheds

We cannot judge a biography by its length, by the number of pages in it; we must judge by the richness of the contents . . . Sometimes the 'unfinisheds' are among the most beautiful symphonies.

Viktor Frankl (1905–97)

Without having lived

To die is poignantly bitter, but the idea of having to die without having lived is unbearable.

Erich Fromm (1900–80)

The two pieces that follow were found on the Compassionate Friends Poetry Corner, a webpage where the bereaved have the opportunity to remember those they have lost through a poem or song. The first piece is dedicated 'For Nick – our very own comet in the night sky', the second 'To Holly who I love and miss so very much'.

Gone Too Soon

Like A Comet
Blazing 'Cross The Evening Sky
Gone Too Soon

Like A Rainbow
Fading In The Twinkling Of An Eye
Gone Too Soon

Shiny And Sparkly
And Splendidly Bright
Here One Day
Gone One Night

Like The Loss Of Sunlight
On A Cloudy Afternoon
Gone Too Soon

Like A Castle
Built Upon A Sandy Beach
Gone Too Soon

Like A Perfect Flower
That Is Just Beyond Your Reach
Gone Too Soon

Born to Amuse, To Inspire, To Delight
Here One Day
Gone One Night

Like A Sunset
Dying With The Rising Of The Moon
Gone Too Soon

Buz Kohan and sung by Michael Jackson

The cord

We are connected,
My child and I, by
An invisible cord
Not seen by the eye.
It's not like the cord
That connects us 'til birth,
This cord can't be seen
By any on Earth.
This cord does its work
Right from the start.

It binds us together
Attached to my heart.
I know that it's there
Though no one can see
The invisible cord
From my child to me.
The strength of this cord
Is hard to describe.
It can't be destroyed
It can't be denied.
It's a cord much stronger than
Man could create.
It withstands the test,
Can hold any weight.
And though you are gone,
And you're not here with me,
The cord is still there
But no one can see.
It pulls at my heart,
I am bruised . . . I am sore,

But this cord is my lifeline
As never before.
I am thankful that God
Connects us this way.
A mother and child
Death can't take away!

Author unknown

PRAYERS

So many hopes

We had so many hopes, so many fears,
there has been so much joy, so much sorrow,
and now all our words seem empty.

What we want we cannot have;
and what we thought was promised
has been taken from us.
O God,
do not let our pain turn to bitterness
that devours us and kills us.
We thank you for all that is good.
Help us to find peace in troubled times,
and light in our darkness.
These things we ask through Jesus Christ our Lord. Amen.

Joint Liturgical Group

Aching hearts

Father God,
who watched your own Son die,
our hearts ache beyond our describing –
they break and we feel beyond all comfort.
The heavens seem shut,
and the earth is a wilderness of sorrow and grief.
With your Son on his cross we cry,
'My God, my God, why have you abandoned me?'

Joint Liturgical Group

Comfort this family

Loving God, our Father,
who has blessed mankind with the gift of family life,
be near to comfort this family,
grieving deeply at the loss of their child.
Help them in their sorrow
to know that in your great love and eternal kingdom
this young and precious life is safe and continuing.
We ask this from the compassion of our hearts,
in the name of Jesus our Saviour and Friend.

David M. Owen

Lord Jesus, take this child

Lord Jesus, take this child,
So briefly in our care,
Into your eternal world
To breathe its purer air.

And, as you shared their grief
Who mourned for Lazarus,
In our own time of sudden loss,
Comfort and strengthen us.

Bless those who seek to heal
All kinds of human pain;
And all who do not lose their faith,
Though mysteries remain.

As praying turns to praise,
Together we adore
The God who wipes away our tears
And bids us grieve no more.

Fred Pratt Green (1903–2000)
Tune: Franconia

The child we have lost

Loving Father, the child we have lost in death was part of us, flesh of our flesh, and we feel bereft and incomplete, like losing a limb that can never be restored.

Help us to trust you for your promise of new life and new beginnings. Reassure us that the words Jesus spoke so long ago, he speaks still: 'Let the children come to me, for the kingdom of heaven is theirs.' And while we wait to meet again in the life after death, help us to live lovingly and happily with the rest of our family.

We pray through him who, from the cross, saw his mother's grief, Jesus Christ our living Lord.

David M. Owen

Sorrowing hearts

O God, our heavenly Father, whose ways are hidden and thy works wonderful, comfort, we pray, this woman and her husband whose hearts are heavy with sorrow. Surround them with thy protection, and grant them grace to face the future with good courage and hope. Teach them to use this pain in deeper sympathy for all who suffer, so that they may share in thy work of turning sorrow into joy; through Jesus Christ our Lord.

The Guild of Health

7

Unable to bear it

———◆◆◆———

They were a happy couple when I married them, but five years later the husband became very depressed and took his own life, leaving his young wife devastated, and his family, friends and work colleagues deeply saddened and wondering what more they could have done to help.

Sadly, news stories of suicides are far too common. People of all ages and professions tragically end their own lives. As I write, within recent months there have been cases of a government scientist and a city lawyer, and several of young people caught up in the pressures on them to succeed. People commit suicide for a number of reasons – old age and the loss of independence and dignity; a terminal illness and the wish to avoid prolonged suffering or being a burden to others; unrelieved physical pain and disability; a shattering failure or disappointment; inability to cope with the demands made of them; bullying at school or in the workplace; aching loneliness following the loss of a loved one or a divorce; the loss of a job with its accompanying stigma and insecurity. And invariably there is depression, characterized by a feeling of worthlessness, helplessness, guilt, loss of appetite and sexual desire, loss of weight, chronic insomnia, apathy and fatigue. The depressed person often withdraws from society and loses interest even in once-prized activities. Suicide is the utterly lonely end of a precious life, brought on by a terrible agony when that agony exceeds the resources to cope. People resort to suicide when they can't bear it any more and have given up hope of being helped.

While the person who has died is relieved of the distress, the agony continues in the lives of his or her loved ones left to mourn. Often they feel guilty at not having done enough, or perhaps because they quarrelled with the person. That the suicide should have happened in their family may result in recriminations. A stony silence on the matter may follow, an unwillingness to talk about it among themselves or to others outside.

Anyone who has had to bear this kind of bereavement will appreciate the need for loving support. Thankfully, Christian opinion has moved from cruel condemnation of those who have taken their own lives to compassion. We may have difficulty in condoning the act, but we are comforted by the approach that reaches out in understanding and acceptance of the distress that has driven a person to such an extremity, for this is a failure to cope with stress and not a sin. The lost loved one should be remembered with gratitude and affection.

People who threaten to take their own lives must be taken seriously. Their threat is a distress signal – a cry for help – and they need skilled counselling and care. But not all the skilled care offered and accepted by a suicidal person removes the need for ordinary compassion – indeed it merely supplements it. An hour spent in company with a friend over a cup of tea, an invitation to a meal, to a car ride in the countryside – just warm, caring friendship – can often work wonders. To love in that kind of way is to walk very close to God.

REFLECTIONS

Expression of distress

In general, the suicidal person is in a disorganized, chaotic state. He feels helpless, hopeless and is looking desperately for assistance. He is usually anxious, confused, and frequently hostile.

He feels lonely, alone, and rejected, and thinks no one loves him. His suicidal behaviour can best be understood as an expression of his severe emotional distress.

Suicide Prevention Centre

Then someone cared

Serena was 16 when, last year, she found herself standing at the top of a multi-storey car park in Hampshire, willing herself to jump off. She is a bright, engaging and cynically funny young woman from a middle-class home but she had spent the previous two years in what she describes as a profound state of 'disconnectedness' from the world. She had become so low that she had ceased to feel anything except a thudding sense of pointlessness . . . One day, when she should have been at school, she walked to the top of the multi-storey car park. 'I think I did want to die,' she says. 'I didn't see myself as being any use to anybody. But then my mate called me on my mobile, and asked why I wasn't at school. It made me think that someone cared, and that stopped me.'

Carol Midgley

Tribulation

The New Testament scholar William Barclay reminds us that the Greek word translated 'tribulation' means 'pressure', and that in classical Greek it is used, for instance, of a man tortured to death by being slowly crushed by a great boulder laid on him. He writes: 'There is the pressure of work, the pressure of worry, the pressure of material circumstances, the pressure of opposition and antagonism and persecution. Under that pressure many people collapse. Life becomes too much for them; physically and mentally they cannot bear the strain.'

I believe that those who in this life find the strain too much are met in death by the mercy of God. We take comfort in that, and trust that those who lost their peace here are at peace in

him, who alone understands the agonies that beset us in this
mortal life.

David M. Owen

The existence of love

I had thought that your death
Was a waste and a destruction,
A pain of grief hardly to be endured.
I am only beginning to learn
That your life was a gift and a growing
And a loving left with me.
The desperation of death
Destroyed the existence of love.
But the fact of death
Cannot destroy what has been given.
I am learning to look at your life again
Instead of your death and your departing.

Marjorie Pizer

PRAYERS

For those who despair

Lord Jesus,
As you bowed your head and died,
A great darkness covered the land.

We lay before you
The despair of all
Who find life
Without meaning or purpose,
And see no value in themselves,
Who suffer the anguish
Of inner darkness
That can only lead them
To self-destruction and death.

Lord,
in your passion, you too
felt abandoned, isolated, derelict.

You are one
With all who suffer
Pain and torment
Of body and mind.

Be to them the light
That has never been mastered.
Pierce the darkness
Which surrounds and engulfs them,
So that they may know
Within themselves
Acceptance, forgiveness, and peace.

We pray for those who,
Through the suicide of one close to them,
Suffer the emptiness of loss
And the burden of untold guilt.
May they know your gift of acceptance,
So that they may be freed
From self-reproach
And mutual recrimination,
And find in the pattern
Of your dying and rising,
New understanding, and purpose
For their lives.

Neville Smith

For those who see no other way

Lord, it's not easy for us who enjoy life and wish it to continue, to understand those who are so depressed they are driven to end it. In your mercy receive those who have died, and uphold in your love others who have attempted suicide but survived.

Give to them the comfort and strength of your presence, and
the gift of caring friends and helpers.

David M. Owen

But she could not pull out of it

We had all felt and seen it coming, Lord. She was so deeply sad,
depressed beyond all human endurance. The doctors tried
drugs and her friends laughter and firmness, patience and
love. But she could not pull out of it. And so she took that over-
dose and died. Well, Lord, I feel in my heart that you could have
boundless love and care and compassion for her and that now
she will never more be depressed, but know the fullness of joy
and peace in you. So thus I pray in confidence, Lord.

Michael Hollings and Etta Gullick

You alone know what he suffered

Lord, we cannot understand why N took his own life. You alone
know what he suffered. Forgive our lack of understanding, and
give him the comfort and compassion which we so unthink-
ingly failed to give. Lord, we pray that he may rest in peace with
you in the warmth of your love; and, Lord, give support to his
family and those close to him through your healing and
redeeming love which you showed us in your Son.

Michael Hollings and Etta Gullick

Come unto me

We remember in the presence of God
Our neighbours who find no purpose in life and no joy
    in living.
Jesus said
    Come unto me.
In the name of Jesus the crucified
We try to imagine the mood of despair
And the hatred of one's own body
Which makes men long for death.

Jesus said
Come unto me.
Many of us have known such moods from time to time.
Perhaps some of us have been near to suicide itself.
Let us be honest with ourselves and with God.
And in our heart of hearts admit to him what we
    painfully try to forget.
Jesus said
Come unto me.
With ourselves let us include in loving prayer
Those we may never meet and do not know
Who hate what they have done or what they are
And who cannot face life any more;
Many in our community, our own street, in our own
    church.
Jesus said
Come unto me.
Lord God, with us or without us,
By your word or by your deed,
Save, and redeem and give them your new life today.
    Amen.

Simon H. Baynes
Based on Matthew 11.28

Christ my helper

You, O Christ, have been there before me.

The darker the torment that drags me down,
    the brighter and higher I rise with you.
The sorer the grief that tears me apart,
    the sweeter the healing and joy you bring.
The stronger the death that locks me fast,
    the surer your Life that sets me free.

Prayer Fellowship Handbook

8

Coping with disaster

————◆◆◆————

Disasters are ever with us – nature's variety of earthquakes, hurricanes, tornadoes, lightning strikes, wildfires, floods and droughts, and the man-made causes of accidents and terrorist atrocities. They devastate countless lives and communities and destroy valuable properties and possessions. Many hundreds of people died in Bangladesh in 1989 from a ferocious tornado, and thousands of others in the Boxing Day 2004 Pacific tsunami, and in 2005 from Hurricane Katrina in New Orleans and the earthquake in Pakistan. Since 1998 more than 30 people have died as a direct result of flooding in Britain alone. Humankind's violence brought death to hundreds in New York in September 2001, and over 50 people died in London in July 2005, victims of terrorism. People die daily in Iraq, Afghanistan, the Middle East and Darfur. People are killed in crowd stampedes, from nuclear accidents, mechanical failures, collapsing buildings. People are killed in sinking ships and crashing aeroplanes. The list is endless.

Disasters kill and maim thousands, leaving trails of destruction. They result in traumatized lives for survivors – sufferers from Post Traumatic Stress Disorder (PTSD) – and in untold grief for relatives and friends. Many who are injured in them recover well and live to help others through similar afflictions, but many lives are permanently blighted by disability, nightmarish recollections and fear. And it is noticeable how disasters invariably throw up the deeply theological question of God's involvement, and therefore of his character.

When a collapsing coal tip engulfed a school at Aberfan in 1966, killing 116 children, one man was heard to respond, 'Where was God when this lot came down?' Behind the question lay either a denial of God's existence, or an assertion that if there was a God, he was unable to control what had happened, or was unaware of it or indifferent to it.

Loss of life or injury as a result of such disasters constitutes the atheist's best weapon of attack against belief in God. How can a God of love in control of his world allow this to happen? Following most tragedies it is our tendency to blame someone. In the case of disease leading to death, or of earthquake, hurricane, flood or drought, who is to blame but God?

People in Old Testament times clearly saw God as the sole Creator of the world, the initiator of all that happens. See, for example, Isaiah 45.7: 'I make the light, I create darkness, author alike of prosperity and trouble. I, the LORD, do all these things' (NEB). They mostly believed too that human disasters were sent by God as punishment for sin, and that he rewarded the righteous with prosperity. The value of the Book of Job lies in its challenge to the easy notion of divine punishment, for Job had lived an upright life, yet had suffered appallingly.

In a sense, all sin brings suffering of a kind. There is the suffering caused by drunken drivers or negligent engineers. In the case of Aberfan there had been prior warnings that the coal tip was dangerous. We cannot flout basic physical or moral laws without consequences. Much suffering is caused by sin, but not all. We have all known saintly people upon whom great personal disaster has fallen – a reminder that sun and rain fall indiscriminately on the just and unjust, on good and bad alike. The righteous have no more immunity against disaster than the unrighteous.

In the New Testament we find Jesus unwilling to accept the traditional glib answers. With reference to the falling tower of Siloam and loss of life (Luke 13.1–5), he repudiates the belief that this disaster was God's punishment for people's sins.

According to the interpretation of one scholar, Jesus is saying in effect, 'We don't know why the Galileans and the eighteen workmen of Siloam died. They were neither better nor worse than their fellows. The real question for us is not why they were taken, but why are we left?'

Jesus' disciples too, in line with Old Testament thinking, posed the same dilemma when confronted with the man born blind: 'Who sinned, this man or his parents, that he was born blind?' (John 9.2 NIV). Jesus refused to relate his blindness to either parent, adding, 'He was born blind so that God's power might be displayed in curing him.' We must not take this to mean that he had suffered his blindness all those years in order that Jesus might perform a miracle of healing that would delight the crowd. Rather, he says, don't question why this man was born blind or who is to blame, ask instead what God is going to do in this situation – the implication being that God wishes to act compassionately on the man's behalf.

Of course we will debate the moral and spiritual implications of tragedies, whether natural or man-made. Human negligence that has brought about someone's death is more clearly defined and dealt with, whereas natural disasters, so-called 'acts of God', can often cause tremors in our faith. But we can be sure of this. It is quite contrary to our Christian belief in a loving Father to say that he releases natural elements like storm or earthquake to hurt or correct us, or that he is unconcerned about us when we are caught up in a disaster. His created world is made up of sunshine, rain and wind, of ocean and landscape, all of which contain elements that are dangerous to us humans, and that require our utmost caution. To provide absolute protection would mean removing us from planet Earth altogether, or else greatly limiting our freedom of movement and choice.

To ask why God allows suffering is quite in order, and even goes some way to answering the problem. We may not say God sends or causes suffering, for this would be to involve him in an absurd contradiction, since our knowledge of him is clearly that he wills the relief of suffering. We are sure that he has granted freedom to his created order in which disasters and sorrows occur (what H. H. Farmer, former Cambridge professor of theology, suggested in his phrase 'the relative independence of the world', meaning that God does not interrupt the process of creation he has set in motion). He has given integrity to nature, and it is within this 'relative independence' that disasters, diseases and accidents occur. We know that God does not want any of us to suffer, for he is on the side of health and happiness.

Let us realize that creation is continuous. God is still at work in evolving his world. The process he began millions of years ago in shaping the earth's crust he continues, even though human beings are on the scene, and are sometimes affected by upheavals in the process. Teilhard de Chardin said, 'In all evolution we have to reckon with failures and mistakes.'

Truly this is life, and we have to accept it. What happens to us here, whether we live for many years or a few, whether in sickness or in health, is an inexplicable fact of creation. While suffering and death will be lessened by taking extra precautions, and indeed by sinning less, they can never be totally avoided. Of course we might suffer less deprivation if we avoid falling in love and getting married and having children, or making friendships or assuming responsibilities, but would we really want this? We who are artists in living must endure the agony if we are to enjoy the ecstasy.

However intense our questioning, we are left with the ever-recurring fact of human tragedies. To blame God is pointless and unnecessary: better to offer him the service of our skills and the generous gifts of our money to help where we can, and be part of his concern to take action. 'Although the world is full of suffering,' wrote Helen Keller, who was blind, deaf and dumb, 'it is also full of the overcoming of it.'

The religion of Jesus calls us to move beyond speculation. It bids us see him both exercising deeds of love toward the needy and, in the cross, involving himself supremely in our human scene, facing the worst that could happen, yet turning history's blackest day into one of brightness and joy.

REFLECTIONS

To live in hope

To live in hope is not to live with a false sense of optimism. Nor is it only the old who are sometimes tempted to despair that the world seems to be governed by fury. The wells of peace are poisoned, the cries of the suffering largely ignored. On the day that the twin towers were demolished, an estimated 35,600 of the world's children died from conditions of starvation.

Yet despair is never an option, and those who follow Christ need to hold in a fine balance two great requirements that our faith lays upon us. The first is that of love: love for the world in all its need, that together we may 'act justly, love mercy, and walk humbly with our God.'

The second is to remember that there is a world elsewhere. The world is truly a place of oppression, poverty, and disease, but that's only half the story. For the horrors of war and the violent acts of the wicked don't abolish beauty, destroy art, overthrow truth, or nullify love and compassion. Yeats wrote of how no man can create like Shakespeare, Homer, or Sophocles, 'who does not believe with all his blood and nerve, that man's soul is immortal.'

Michael Mayne (1929–2006)

Ground Zero

To look upon Ground Zero is an intensely moving experience. Children's paintings articulate the loss of their parents (often fire fighters): grief, pain, anger, bewilderment – they're all there. There was scarcely a dry eye in the crowd. A few yards away lies St. Paul's chapel, an offshoot of Trinity, Wall Street. In addition to daily worship, the chapel is given over to an interactive

exhibition that features messages from around the world, showing solidarity with the people of New York.
. . . A public tragedy calls for public symbols and places to grieve. These enable people individually and collectively to remember, to own their grief, to mourn. Only then will they grieve healthily and start to reconstruct their lives.

Frances Bridger

What sort of world?

We may not say that God 'creates' moral evil, though we have to admit that he permits it and to that extent has some responsibility for it. But what would we have? It is conceivable that God might have created the entire world a garden of Eden, a ready-made and perfect welfare state, with no crafty serpent and no ravening carnivores to spoil it. Such a world would not be a better world than the world we know. Instead of being moral agents, capable of doing right and wrong, we should have been automata. Better than that, the world as it is, for all its guilt and shame. The world which God created is a world in which there is the constant tension of opposites, light and darkness, weal and woe, good and evil.

C. R. North

No intervention

'Why doesn't God *stop* evil and cruel men from causing so much suffering?' This is a very natural and understandable question, but how exactly could such intervention be arranged without interfering with the gift of personal choice? Are we to imagine the possessor of a cruel tongue to be struck dumb, the writer of irresponsible and harmful newspaper articles visited with writer's cramp, or the cruel and vindictive husband to find himself completely paralysed? Even if we limit God's intervention to the reinforcement of the voice of conscience, what can be done where conscience is disregarded or has been silenced through persistent suppression? The moment we begin to envisage such interventions, the whole structure of human free will is destroyed.

J. B. Phillips (1906–82)

Pattern and illumination

I think it is part of the pattern of life. What's more I think it's an essential part. Imagine human life being drained of suffering! If you could find some means of doing that, you would not ennoble it; you would demean it. Everything I have learnt, whatever it may be – very little I fear – has been learnt through suffering.

Malcolm Muggeridge (1903–90)

To God we cried

> The storm upon us fell,
> The floods around us rose;
> The depths of death and hell
> Seemed on our souls to close;
> To God we cried in strong despair,
> He heard, and came to help our prayer.

Henry Francis Lyte (1793–1847)
Based on Psalm 18

God in the midst

Ernest Gordon has written of his experience in a Burma death camp. There in the squalor and starvation, where demoralized prisoners were dying like flies, a little group of men – none of them churchmen or believers, not even Gordon himself – began to read the New Testament.

Gordon writes: 'In the light of our new understanding, the Crucifixion was seen as being of the utmost relevance to our situation. A God who remained indifferent to the plight of his creatures was not a God with whom we could agree. The Crucifixion, however, told us that God was in our midst, suffering with us . . . We could see that God was not indifferent to such suffering. We stopped complaining about our own. Faith could not save us from it, but it would take us through it. We looked at the cross and took strength from the knowledge that it gave us, that God was in our midst.'

Gordon cannot explain why men have to suffer as they do. . . . Nor can I. But we know the place where we can learn what matters more – how to meet it and how it can be used. And we offer to you the Person through whose pain we find the way to God, for it was God's way to us. 'Christ also hath once suffered for our sins, the just for the unjust, that he might bring us to God.'

David H. C. Read (1910–2001)

PRAYERS

Following a natural disaster

Where, O God, were you?
Did you not care?
Have you hidden from us all hope and believing?

Our hearts and minds reel,
Our thoughts and speech outrun reason
And we cry out in pain.
O God, where are you?
Do not hide your face from us.
Do not leave us without comfort or solace.

When we run to the ends of the earth,
When we rage in the dark of the night,
Meet us there
And grant us peace, and hope enough
To entrust N to you.
With all who suffer today we cry to you.

Lord, in your mercy,
Hear our prayer.

Joint Liturgical Group

Following a disaster arising from human error or accident

> Suddenly, O God,
> We have lost *the one/those* we love.
> In hurt, in anger, in despair,
> Meet us where we are.
>
> We long for answers,
> To learn and put right what we can.
> May the truth set us free.
>
> Give us courage to bear what cannot be undone.
> Comfort us and all who mourn with us.
>
> For *N and all who have suffered*
> We make our prayers.
> Bring *them* by your mercy to that place where
>   suffering is no more.
> This we ask through Jesus Christ, your Son, our
>   Lord. Amen.

Joint Liturgical Group

Someone to blame

Lord, so many things have gone wrong in our lives and in the world; so many disasters and sorrows, and we needed some-one to blame, so we blamed you. Looking back, we know now that we were thoughtless in this, and really did ourselves no good since you want only the best for us. Sorry, Lord. Please forgive us.

David M. Owen

Why, Lord?

O Creator of the universe, when earthquakes, cyclones, floods and droughts strike we ask why?
Why, if you are loving as well as all-powerful,
did you create a world in which these disasters happen
and innocent people suffer so helplessly?

To that question we can give no answer.
Faith says, God knows.
He made the world and pronounced it good
and in Christ he suffers with us.

We praise you, suffering Father of Jesus,
for your grace shown in those whose faith remains firm
when disasters destroy all their possessions
and even their loved ones;

For your grace shown in those whose love remains sure,
who are concerned with others, who put themselves last;
for your grace in those who offer help,
who leave comfort and work long hours in tough conditions
to relieve suffering, we praise you.

Prayer Fellowship Handbook

The hospital

Lord, suffering disturbs me, oppresses me.
I don't understand why you allow it.
Why, Lord?

Why this innocent child who has been moaning for a week,
    horribly burned?
This man who has been dying for three days and three
    nights, calling for his mother?
This woman with cancer who in one month seems ten
    years older?
This worker fallen from his scaffolding, a broken puppet
    less than twenty years old?
This stranger, poor isolated wreck, who is one great open
    sore?
This woman in a cast, lying on a board for more than
    thirty years?
Why, Lord?
I don't understand.

Why this suffering in the World that shocks, isolates,
  revolts, shatters?
Why this hideous suffering that strikes blindly without
  seeming cause,
Falling unjustly on the good, and sparing the evil,
Which seems to withdraw, conquered by science, but comes
  back in another form, more powerful and more subtle?
I don't understand.
Suffering is odious and frightens me.
Why these people, Lord, and not others?
Why these, and not me?

Son, it is not I, your God, who has willed suffering, it is
  men.
They have brought it into the world in bringing sin,
Because sin is disorder, and disorder hurts.
There is for every sin, somewhere in the world and in time,
  a corresponding suffering.

But I came, and I took all your sufferings upon me, as I
  took all your sins,
I took them and suffered them before you.
I transformed them, I made of them a treasure.
They are still evil, but an evil with a purpose,
For through your sufferings, I accomplish redemption.

Michel Quoist

9

The cost of war

———◆◆———

Early in the Second World War my uncle, who was a pilot officer, and his crew were shot down over Germany. I was only eight years old at the time but I still remember the grief-stricken faces of my grandparents when they received the news that their son was 'missing, believed killed'. For some time they clung to the faint hope that he had not lost his life, and was a prisoner of war, but their worst fears were eventually confirmed. It was a shattering blow that they never really got over.

They were just two parents among thousands to suffer such a stunning loss. Near where I lived as a boy were two young brothers. Both lost their lives in the war when their ship was torpedoed, leaving their parents doubly devastated. A woman described to me the loss of her son in war as 'worse than losing a limb'. A nation at war is a nation of countless broken hearts and ruined lives.

People who lose a loved one in war often agonize over whether or not his or her death was worthwhile. To lose someone in a 'just war' for reasons of self-defence brings some reassurance at least to the bereaved, whereas to lose someone in a war they deem futile carries a more bitter sting. During a two months' stay in the United States shortly after the Vietnam War, I met with a great deal of resentment at America's involvement, which had resulted in appalling loss of life, and we have seen this again in the USA and the UK following the war in Iraq.

Among the sorrows of war is the inability of grieving relatives to bury their dead. Some are interred in war graves, later to be visited, but as many again perish without trace. My uncle's body was never found; the most that could be granted was the inscription of his name among thousands of his Air Force compatriots at the Runnymede memorial, and at the war memorial in his home town.

Public cenotaphs are of great importance. It is true most of us pass them by without a thought except for the annual occasion of Remembrance Sunday, too busy to recall their significance; but they bear a timeless recollection of our conflicts, 'lest we forget', and symbolize our longing for peace 'when war shall be no more'.

They are reminders in stone of the tragic loss of life during the past century and into the present. In the 1914–18 war, 'the war to end all wars', 8.5 million members of the forces of all nations are said to have perished, and 21 million to have been wounded. The Second World War was even more devastating, with 22 million military and civilian dead and 34 million wounded. It was the war in which the Nazis exterminated six million Jews – a crime that has defiled the world. Anyone who visits Yad Vashem in Jerusalem, the memorial to the Holocaust, will have its horrors painfully brought home. I stood one day in its Hall of Remembrance, before the Eternal Flame and the names of the 21 death camps. Beside me stood a woman, frail and weeping. As I turned to her she told me in her anguish, simply, 'I was at Auschwitz.' As she went away and mingled again with the crowd, what brutality I wondered had she seen, what fear, what awful death, what personal loss? My eyes filled with tears as she brought home to me in that unforgettable moment the bitter pangs of war.

Since those terrible years there has been conflict in Korea, Vietnam, Afghanistan (as there still is today), the Falklands, Northern Ireland, and the Middle East. The Israelis and Palestinians are in constant and bitter dispute, and Iraq has been plunged into chaos following two wars. Brutalities continue in Sudan as in other parts of the African continent. In all of these conflicts, and in many others, there has been a huge loss of life among the armed forces and civilians which needs to be part of our acts of remembrance.

Let our memorials in stone, our plaques in public places, our Remembrance Day services go on reminding us of the sorrows of war and the cost of our conflicts in terms of human life. Let them be symbols of our resolve, for to remember the dead without striving to act as peacemakers in our relationships is to dishonour them. Let our memorials tell of courage and sacrifice, and of a tomorrow better than yesterday; let them depict the cross of Christ, with all its shame, and in all its glory.

REFLECTIONS

Known unto God

He was also given an identification disc, what my generation of American war-movie viewers would call a 'dog-tag', giving his name, army number and religion. Here at a stroke was the fighting man's best hope of being identified – and remembered – in death. Before the dog-tags a man killed in battle might never be identified, even with the best will in the world. There are lots of stories of soldiers in the American Civil War carrying notes in their pockets bearing the handwritten details of their identities: if you find me when I'm dead, this is who I am.

At the start of the Great War, soldiers wore a single red circular disc made of vulcanised fibre. During the carnage of the Somme, these were collected from the dead – for the combined purpose of having the relevant details to send a letter home to the family and to ensure his pay was promptly stopped. The army didn't pay wages to dead soldiers. This practice, logical enough at the time and in the desperately confusing circumstances, caused problems later on. By the time there was a sufficient break in the fighting to allow for collection and burial of the dead, the decomposing and therefore unrecognisable bodies were no longer identifiable. This is part of the explanation for the legend 'The Missing of the Somme' that appears on the memorial at Thiepval. Having earlier collected the red identity discs, they knew who was dead; the problem was they could no longer connect the names they had to the bodies. It was for this reason that so many graves had to be marked:

A SOLDIER OF THE GREAT WAR KNOWN UNTO GOD

It was also behind the decision to create the haunting memorials such as Thiepval, the Menin Gate and Tyne Cot, bearing lists of names of men known to have died but whose actual resting place could not be identified.

Neil Oliver

The Unknown Warrior

That Unknown Warrior, selected with such determined anonymity at St-Pol, was carried across France with full battle honours. At the port of Boulogne the first coffin was placed inside a second that had been made from oak brought over especially from Hampton Court. A sixteenth-century crusader's sword was mounted on top and the whole lot was wrapped in the Union Jack – the same one used as an altar cloth throughout the war by the Reverend Railton, whose idea it had been originally. Taken aboard the French destroyer *Verdun*, the coffin was brought to England and put aboard a special train bound for London's Victoria Station. On arrival, at platform 8, the coffin was placed on a catafalque where it remained overnight under the protection of an honour guard. The following day, November 11th 1920, it was loaded on to a gun carriage pulled by six black, plumed horses and taken to Whitehall, where, at eleven o'clock, the newly completed cenotaph was revealed. A two-minute silence began.

Neil Oliver

Courage in duty

It never ceases to amaze me what our servicemen have done, and continue to do, for their country and their comrades. Their courageous acts in the line of duty are humbling for us all; I and many others are immensely proud of them.

The briefings by the Commanding Officers of the regiments of which I am Colonel-in-Chief on their return from operations, and the stories told to me by 'The Old and Bold' of battles long ago, are wonderfully inspiring; the stoicism and great good humour with which they have dealt with unimaginably awful situations is deeply moving. In troops and platoons, ships and aircraft, and individually, they have carried out acts of immense bravery; yet to a man they are modest and self-effacing.

Over the years, and particularly as President of the Victoria Cross and George Cross Association, in succession to my grandmother, Queen Elizabeth the Queen Mother, I have met many of these remarkable men and women and can understand only too well why they have meant so much to my family over the years.

The Prince of Wales

A widow's wreath

Some elements of the Remembrance Sunday service at the Cenotaph will always remain constant: the haunting rendition of Nimrod by the massed bands, the observance of the two minutes' silence and the warm applause that accompanies the veterans' march past.

But the simple passage of time dictates that not everything can stay the same.

None of the handful of surviving First World War veterans was in Whitehall yesterday. But, for the first time, an army wife widowed by the war in Iraq attended to lay a wreath.

Raqual Harper-Titchener, 31, placed her wreath of fallen oak leaves in memory of all service personnel killed on duty since the end of the Second World War. The wreath – 'fallen leaves for the fallen' – was placed on the Cenotaph alongside the traditional red poppy tributes left by the Queen, the Prime Minister, other dignitaries and veterans' associations.

Mrs. Harper-Titchener's husband, Matthew, 32, a major in the Royal Military Police, was killed in August 2003 when she was pregnant with their second child. This was the first time that she had attended the ceremony at the Cenotaph.

'I felt very tearful,' she said. 'The silence and the march past really affected me. Even though it was a big public occasion I felt I was very much on my own. I kind of disappeared into myself.'

Sean O'Neill

The family

We weren't called the Army, we were called the family, and that is what it felt like. I hope generations to come continue to remember what men sacrificed for their country.

Walter Rookes (80), Second World War veteran

Jesus, make it stop

> Lines of grey, muttering faces, masked with fear,
> They leave their trenches, going over the top,
> While time ticks blank and busy on their wrists,
> And hope, with furtive eyes and grappling fists,
> Flounders in mud, O Jesus, make it stop!

Siegfried Sassoon (1886–1967)

Prayer: sacred and profane

There are circumstances in which words are as empty as the Cenotaph on Whitehall. I am not alone in having experienced – through illness and grief, for example – situations in which the only prayer I can muster is an animal cry, a groan aimed wildly towards heaven.

At the same time, like most people in the UK today, I have not experienced the terror of bombardment, the intense second-by-second violence that can be found in a war zone. Yet it remains commonplace in too many places in the world.

I believe terror, intense pain, and wild grief share similar features: they are places where, because of their severity, the easy words fail, leaving us with questions such as these: beyond the wordless cry, what words will suffice for prayer under extreme conditions? And can prayer properly be spoken there?

In times of anxiety and pain, I know many have found the Psalms enormously comforting, but they have rarely helped me in the midst of agony or fear – in the very moment when I've been assaulted by the pain my chronic ill-health has sometimes thrown at me. Under such circumstances, Sassoon's 'O Jesus, make it stop!' (with the occasional addition of suitable expletives) have been the only words substantial enough to take the weight of prayer.

I sense they have been the words of countless people down the centuries, caught in situations of intense need, in which our usual pious formulations seem as substantial as the promises of a tyrant. Sassoon wrote those words as the closing line of a poem about a trench attack in a now ancient war, the Great War; yet because they were generated out of experience *in extremis*, they retain the power to speak into human extremes.

I do not think that it is cheap to say that one does not have to have experienced being shelled on the Western Front, or in Bosnia, Iraq, Lebanon, or Israel, to know times when 'hope, with furtive eyes and grappling fists, Flounders in mud', and the only prayerful Christian response is 'O Jesus, make it stop!'

Another poet of the Great War, Wilfred Owen, claimed: 'There is a point where prayer is indistinguishable from blasphemy, There is also a point where blasphemy is indistinguishable from prayer.' I read these words as saying that, in some extreme circumstances, the sacred and profane meet and embrace.

This embrace is often a wordless cry. 'O Jesus, make it stop!' gives words for that cry. Its direct, terse nature makes it almost an expletive, a prayerful swearword. Indeed, the 'O Jesus' has both the feel of a petition and the edge of the modern-day usage heard every day on our streets as a throwaway expletive. To try to offer to God anything more nuanced in times of abject pain, terror or fear would be an attempt to soften reality. The dreadfulness of pain and the dignity of the sufferer demand words as immediate and as sincere as Sassoon gives us.

Rachel Mann

War memorials

War memorials are a familiar sight in the landscape of the United Kingdom. They provide insight into not only the changing face of commemoration, but also military history, social history, and art history. There are an estimated 70,000 war memorials throughout the UK in many different forms, from the frequently seen community crosses or plaques, to buildings, lichgates, gardens, hospitals, organs, chapels and windows.

The United Kingdom National Inventory
of War Memorials

Suicide in the trenches

> I knew a simple soldier boy
> Who grinned at life in empty joy,
> Slept soundly through the lonesome dark,
> And whistled early with the lark.
>
> In winter trenches, cowed and glum,
> With crumps and lice and lack of rum,
> He put a bullet through his brain.
> No one spoke of him again.
>
> You smug-faced crowds with kindling eye
> Who cheer when soldier lads march by,

Sneak home and pray you'll never know
The hell where youth and laughter go.

Siegfried Sassoon (1886–1967)

What, for those who die?

What passing-bells for those who die as cattle?
Only the monstrous anger of the guns.
Only the stuttering rifles' rapid rattle
Can patter out their hasty orisons.
No mockeries now for them; no prayers nor bells;
Nor any voice of mourning save the choirs,
The shrill, demented choirs of wailing shells;
And bugles calling for them from sad shires.

What candles may be held to speed them all?
Not in the hand of boys, but in their eyes
Shall shine the holy glimmers of goodbyes.
The pallor of girls' brows shall be their pall;
Their flowers the tenderness of patient minds,
And each slow dusk a drawing-down of blinds.

Wilfred Owen (1893–1918)

They died for us

We want to live. We did not ask to be born into a world of guns and bombs. We do not want to fight. Leave us alone, you statesmen and rulers, let us live our lives in peace. We want to live.

So did they, the boys, girls, men and women who lived, suffered and died in the wars. Of course they wanted to go on living; and yet, for some strange, inscrutable reason that God alone knows, they were destined for wounds and slaughter. God let them be killed. Before they died, many of them had to endure hell on earth. Somehow they struggled on. Where did they find the strength? Some, in the people they loved, or the country they loved, or the sheer animal will to survive; some, in their faith in God.

There were those who believed that they were giving themselves to build a world for us. They died for the future, for an ideal world that we could live in, an earth at peace. Now it is our turn to strive for peace on earth. War is not only made by statesmen. It is made by us, ordinary people who strive to achieve our own selfish ends, quarrelling and hating as we pursue our petty, sordid, self-seeking quest. We *can* make peace, with God's help, if we have faith, and hope, and love for one another. *We* are responsible for peace. Let us begin here, to build what the dead of the wars left unfinished. Perhaps we were not worth dying for: but without their sacrifice we would not be alive today.

Let us thank God for them, and let us honour them, in silence.

Michael Davis

We will remember them

> They shall not grow old, as we that are left grow old:
> Age shall not weary them, nor the years condemn.
> At the going down of the sun and in the morning
> We will remember them.

Laurence Binyon (1869–1943)

PRAYERS

Honouring those who died

Grant peace and eternal rest to all the departed, but especially to the millions known and unknown who died as prisoners in many lands, victims of the hatred and cruelty of man. May the example of their suffering and courage draw us closer to thee through thine own agony and passion, and thus strengthen us in our desire to serve thee in the sick, the unwanted and the dying wherever we may find them. Give us grace so to spend ourselves for those who are still alive, that we may prove most truly that we have not forgotten those who have died.

Sue Ryder (1923–2000) and Leonard Cheshire (1917–92)

From war to peace

A hymn for Remembrance Sunday (based on Isaiah 2.2–4; Micah 4.1–3):

The time will come when God's own house
Shall deck the highest hill,
And all the nations of the earth
Shall seek his peaceful will;
'Let us arise', will be their cry,
'To meet our God today,
There we shall learn his perfect truth,
And walk his chosen way.'

Then will our God be arbiter
For nations in dispute,
His righteous judgements once declared
We shall no more refute;
Then will the swords be turned to ploughs,
The spear to pruning-blade,
When human races live as one
With man no more afraid.

We pray, our God, bring near that day
When wars and tumults cease,
Strengthen resolve within our hearts
To fill the world with peace;
To turn all hatred into love,
All weapons that destroy
To implements that build and serve,
And nobler skills employ.

David M. Owen
Suggested tune: Ellacombe

For victims of war

Lord, keep alive in us gratitude to all in the armed services who lost their lives in wars and other conflicts, and help us to honour them by living as peacemakers in all our relationships. Hear us as we pray for those who suffer as a result of war, for the injured, disabled and mentally distressed, for the homeless and refugees, for those who have lost their livelihood and security, and for any who have been left to mourn the death of their loved ones.

David M. Owen

For all who suffer

O God our Father, we bring to you in our prayers those who suffer in body or mind as a result of wars, or because of the fear and suspicions that separate nation from nation, race from race, and man from man.

We pray also for all refugees, and for those who have lost wife or husband, children or parents, livelihood, security, or home.

Have mercy upon them, O God, and prosper all who seek to help them in their need, for the sake of Jesus Christ our Lord.

Frank Colquhoun

For those of ill-will

In Ravensbruch concentration camp during the Second World War an unknown soldier is said to have written this prayer on a torn scrap of paper, and left it beside the body of a dead child:

O Lord, remember not only the men and women of good will, but also those of ill-will. But do not remember all the suffering they have inflicted on us; remember the fruits we have brought, thanks to this suffering – our comradeship, our loyalty, our humility, our courage, our generosity, the greatness of heart which has grown out of all this, and when they come to judgement, let all the fruits which we have borne be their forgiveness.

10

Solace in grief

———◆◆◆———

Not one of us goes through life without suffering the loss of a loved one. The experience, of course, varies according to the relationship we had, the circumstances surrounding the death – whether the one who died was elderly and ill for a long time or young and suddenly taken – and also on the type of person we are, and what inner resources we have to cope with our loss.

In the case of intense grief there are some common features of behaviour. A sudden death causes a terrible shock and a feeling of unreality. We can't believe it's true; it's like a nightmare from which we long to wake up. We may find ourselves looking for the deceased, or imagining when we hear a knock on the door that he or she has returned. There are often feelings of anger and the urge to blame someone, if not for causing the death (which is often the case), then for not doing enough to prevent it – ambulance workers, doctors, hospitals, even God. Strangely, we may even feel angry at our loved one for having left us without warning and in such sorrow. We can be indignant with relatives and friends, and sharp with those who try to help us.

And there are feelings of guilt – perhaps due to a quarrel we never had the chance to make up, or those times during an exhausting period of nursing when we were irritable and said unkind things we never really meant. We feel guilty because we lacked enough sympathy and should have done more, and now these memories come back to haunt us. If only we had a chance to say we are sorry! It's hard to see when our heart is breaking with grief that these feelings, which seem to be so negative, are really expressions of our deep love. One day they will fit into place.

Loneliness is the mother of agonies, and bereavement brings it home like nothing else. Lives that once were intertwined are now severed. The bereaved sometimes say their condition is like an amputation – a part of them is missing. There is now a gap, an emptiness – the empty chair, the empty bed, the empty house we come back to. A widow is no more a wife. 'We' has suddenly become 'I', and 'ours', 'mine'. Jobs that a loved one did or that were done together have now to be done alone, and hands must turn to unfamiliar things. Sadly, to the pain of loneliness is often added the apathy of relatives and friends who forsake us when we need them most, unable perhaps to relate to us in our present distress. Also families today are more scattered than ever, making regular visits difficult, and in many cases impossible.

Grieving is terribly painful, and often lengthy. It can affect us physically, with tightness in the throat, shortness of breath, emptiness in the stomach, loss of weight and lack of sleep. For a while we are in a mental vacuum, with normal life disrupted, and spiritually we may feel distant from God. At times we may feel we are losing our mind, and may perhaps yearn to die and be with our loved one.

Recovery takes time and cannot be rushed. Tears will play a large part in the process, and we must not be ashamed of them or embarrassed at breaking down in front of others. Suppression of grief can cause lasting damage. But we must try to avoid self-pity, which is destructive of healing and repellent to our family and friends. It is a natural inclination to feel sorry for ourselves, but unchecked it can lead to excessive mourning. So there is a balance to keep. When C. S. Lewis's wife died he went through a period of indulgence in self-pity. When he eventually recovered from mourning her death he realized he could then remember her better. Excessive grief, he believed, does not link us to our dead but cuts us off from them. We do well to set his thoughts before us as a goal to aim for.

Meanwhile, we must patiently live through our sorrow, accepting help and friendship when it is offered and needed. It is important to keep up interests in life outside ourselves and our home, and here the Christian Church, with its spiritual teaching and caring fellowship, is of invaluable assistance. One day we may feel better, the next day somewhat worse, but the process of healing has begun. Just as a broken limb needs time to heal, and a festering wound must be cleansed before recovery, so with a broken heart.

REFLECTIONS

Growing stronger

In many respects, then, grief can be regarded as an illness. But it can also bring strength. Just as broken bones may end up stronger than unbroken ones, so the experience of grieving can strengthen and bring maturity to those who have previously been protected from misfortune. The pain of grief is just as much a part of life as the joy of love; it is, perhaps, the price we pay for love, the cost of commitment. To ignore this fact, or to pretend that it is not so, is to put on emotional blinkers which leave us unprepared for the losses that will inevitably occur in our lives and unprepared to help others to cope with the losses in theirs.

Colin Murray Parkes

Grief – what does it do?

Why does grief hurt so much? What does it do to you at its most intense time?

Grief plunges you into an unreal world in which you feel a stranger, unaccustomed to being alone, and with little sense of purpose or direction. You'll probably think it would be nice just to curl up, go to sleep and die.

Grief makes you feel you're the only one around who has lost a loved one, and that all activity ought to cease, and everybody mourn for *you*, for only *you* matter, and it's thoughtless of the world to carry on as normal! If you're elderly you may be glad of the fact – at least there'll not be too many years left in which to bear the pain of separation! If younger you may feel cheated at losing one who should have been your companion for many years.

Grief tempts you to dissociate yourself from outsiders so that you can be alone and cry alone. You're afraid to indulge in conversation, knowing that you will burst into tears and be an embarrassment. Putting on the 'stiff upper lip' is an act you don't feel up to, at least not yet. A widowed person in amongst married couples may feel an added sense of loss.

Grief brings on indecisiveness. Alone at home, you must go out, but when you're out you want to get back to the comfort of familiar things, although you know you are returning to an unwelcoming silence. You may not feel like eating, your appetite gone, or you can't be bothered to prepare much of a meal for yourself. Adversely you may be inclined to 'comfort eat' or drink too much so as to divert the pain for a while.

Grief convulses you when you hold or look at something that your loved one held dear, or perhaps had made, or painted. A photograph of happy times evokes lovely memories, but brings floods of tears. Grief makes you cry when you see other people crying, for now their pain touches your heart as never before. Grief makes you wonder if you will ever find happiness again – but you will, for grief diminishes in time to be replaced by a calmness of mind and heart, and bit by bit, a smile and even a laugh. It is the healing of the heart, and you will want to live on as fully as you can by way of tribute to your beloved.

David M. Owen

To a grieving friend

Dear S . . . Christmas approaches, and amidst the celebrations and greetings, there lies the grieving heart of one who has lost a loved one. The first Christmas is particularly painful in this respect, and takes some getting through, so I have you much in mind and in prayer. You will be helped to see it through and into next year, and the pain will ease little by little, though interspersed by many hours of tears. That's how it is with those of us who have had to say goodbye to the dearest one in our lives. I think the ache in the heart will always be there as a lasting sign of a profound love. We cannot forget: we don't wish to. We have to hold our loved ones within us for the duration of life – and then will come the 'life to come' in the risen Lord, and all will be well. Such a celebration awaits us!

David M. Owen

Rebirth

I am emerging from an ocean of grief,
From the sorrow of many depths,
From the inevitability of tragedy,
From the losing of love,
From the terrible triumph of destruction.
I am seeing the living that is to be lived,
The laughter that is to be laughed,
The joy that is to be enjoyed,
The living that is to be accomplished.
I am learning at last
The tremendous triumph of life.

Marjorie Pizer

Towards meaningfulness

The removal of a loved companion renders life meaningless, at least for a considerable period, until one has regained one's bearings and begun to see the path ahead. Life that is tolerable must be imbued with purpose to give it meaning. The human mind cannot tolerate meaninglessness, for a meaningless life can assume a quality of non-existence that seems worse than death itself. For death is the great unknown experience which may conceivably open up a new vista of fulfilment, whereas the interminable misery of a mortal life that is purposeless and devoid of growth is something that can scarcely be contemplated in normal consciousness. How can one proceed with living in such circumstances? This is the valley of the shadow of death, cold and featureless, that is mentioned in Psalm 23. Until one knows its contours and extent as well as one does one's native domain, one has not tasted life fully. The end is a changed person, one who loves the transpersonal life, whose perspectives are no longer limited to human objectives but are infused with divine forebodings.

Martin Israel (1927–2007)

The sharing of grief

I cannot carry this burden alone, the road is too steep
   and the pain too great.
I shall only get to the top of the hill if I am able to lean
   on a firm shoulder
whose strength lies in the reality of the feet which bear
   its weight.
The sharing of grief is the only solution to the crisis that
   surrounds bereavement in our age.
To share a person's sorrow is to accept their reality and to
   acknowledge
the fact that none of us is immune from death.

Simon Stephens, founder of
The Compassionate Friends

But let me go

Miss me, but let me go.
When I come to the end of the road

And the sun has set for me,
I want no tears in a gloom-filled room,
Why cry for a soul set free?

Miss me a little, but not too long,
And not with your head bowed low.
Remember the love that we once shared.
Miss me, but let me go.

For this is a journey we all must take,
And all must go alone.
It's all part of the Master's plan,
A step on the road to home.

When you are lonely and sick of heart,
Go to the friends we know,
And bury your sorrow in doing good works.
Miss me, but let me go.

Author unknown

Healing time

Time makes everything smooth in the end. Brittle, broken
points of pain and grief cannot last; they are made fragile by
their sharpness. Our memories of hurt must lose their jagged
edges, not because we forget, but because we love. This is part
of what love does. This is the final gift to be had from having
loved and been loved in return. 'It is the function of the brain
to enable us not to remember, but to forget.'

Neil Oliver

But how did he live?

Not, how did he die, but how did he live?
Not, what did he gain, but what did he give?
These are the units to measure the worth
Of a man as a man, regardless of birth.
Not what was his church, nor what was his creed?

But had he befriended those really in need?
Was he ever ready, with a word of good cheer,
To bring back a smile, to banish a tear?
Not what did the sketch in the newspaper say,
But how many were sorry when he passed away?

Author unknown

Afterglow

I'd like the memory of me
To be a happy one.
I'd like to leave an afterglow
Of smiles when life is done.
I'd like to leave an echo
Whispering softly down the ways,
Of happy times and laughing times
And bright and sunny days.
I'd like the tears of those who grieve
To dry before the sun
Of happy memories
That I leave when life is done.

Author unknown

Life goes on

If I should go before the rest of you
Break not a flower nor inscribe a stone,
Nor when I'm gone speak in a Sunday voice
But be the usual selves that I have known,
Weep if you must,
Parting is hell,
But life goes on,
So sing as well.

Joyce Grenfell (1910–79)

Living in laughter

His laughter was better than birds in the morning, his smile
Turned the edge of the wind; his memory
Disarms death and charms the surly grave.
Early he went to bed, too early we
Saw his light put out; yet we should not grieve
More than a little while,
For he lives in the earth around us, laughs from the sky.

C. Day Lewis (1904–72)

Living through the night

He who wants to enjoy the glory of the sunrise must live through the night.

Author unknown

The feel of grief

No one ever told me that grief felt so much like fear. I am not afraid, but the sensation is like being afraid. The same fluttering in the stomach, the same restlessness, the yawning. I keep on swallowing.

At other times it feels like being mildly drunk, or concussed. There is a sort of invisible blanket between the world and me. I find it hard to take in what anyone says. Or perhaps, hard to want to take it in. It is so uninteresting. Yet I want the others to be about me. I dread the moments when the house is empty. If only they would talk to one another and not to me...

And grief still feels like fear. Perhaps, more strictly, like suspense. Or like waiting; just hanging about waiting for something to happen. It gives life a permanently provisional feeling. It doesn't seem worth starting anything. I can't settle down. I yawn, I fidget, I smoke too much. Up till this I always had too little time. Now there is nothing but time. Almost pure time, empty successiveness... Grief is like a long valley, a winding

valley where any bend may reveal a totally new landscape. As
I've already noted, not every bend does. Sometimes the surprise
is the opposite one; you are presented with exactly the same
sort of country you thought you had left behind miles ago. That
is when you wonder whether the valley isn't a circular trench.
But it isn't. There are partial recurrences, but the sequence
doesn't repeat.

C. S. Lewis (1898–1963)

As when they were alive

People do not die for us immediately, but remain bathed in a
sort of *aura* of life which bears no relation to true immortality but through which they continue to occupy our thoughts as
when they were alive. It is as though they were travelling
abroad.

Marcel Proust (1871–1922)

The price we pay

Joys are short-lived, ephemeral;
Sorrows remain, stubbornly
Hurting the heart – the price
We pay for loving and losing.

David M. Owen

When I've gone

When I've gone –
No black clothes,
No black words,
No black looks,
No mourning.
Keep it light,
Keep it bright.
I die,
Don't cry,

I'm fine –
That's why!

David M. Owen

A kind of dying

Grieving for a loved one is a kind of dying. For a while laughter is banished, joy is suspended and contentment a stranger. Hope too is far distant and faith a struggle. Only love is constant, keeping the soul from going under. Life keeps on living while love remains. Love is the greatest, and love is resurrection.

David M. Owen

A day of remembering

I knew a man who died on Easter Sunday; another on Christmas Day; a mother who died on her daughter's birthday, and a man who died on the first day of his retirement. Four British soldiers, among them a woman, were killed in Iraq on Remembrance Sunday 2006.

There is an added poignancy, I think, when that doubly special day comes round as an anniversary, and yet any day on which a loved one has died becomes 'special' for those who grieve. And it is a day for the rest of us to remember, and a thoughtfully worded card or letter, a telephone call or a bunch of flowers and a visit – any one of these becomes a means of God's grace to the grieving, and we too become more special as a thoughtful friend.

David M. Owen

The photograph

I cherish it, *my Love*,
The dearest love I knew;
I hold it to my heart –
The photograph of you.

David M. Owen

The weeping edge

> Grief
> Is the weeping edge of emotion,
> The over-filled vessel ready to spill,
> The flooding river waiting to burst.
> In time it recedes,
> But you can never be sure it won't rise again.

David M. Owen

A brutal and terrible loss

In January 2006 a city lawyer, Thomas ap Rhys Price, 31, was making his way home to his fiancée Adele Eastman, 32, when he was viciously knifed and killed by two hooded youths (Carty and Brown), who had terrorized other people in northwest London. They were caught, convicted and sentenced to life imprisonment in November 2006, but showed no remorse for their terrible crime.

Following their sentencing, Adele Eastman wrote a statement which was read in court and printed in The Times *(and other newspapers) the following day. The description of her deep grief touched millions, and in a way echoes the devastation of all others who suffer the excruciating loss of a loved one whose life is brutally destroyed, and indeed of the awful plight of all of us who try to cope with the heart-rending pain of loss.*

The following is part of Adele Eastman's statement:

I must start by saying that my sense of pain and horror at losing Tom, and in such a brutal way, is literally indescribable. I have found it almost impossible even to try to put it into words, but hope that I manage to convey it at least to some extent through my statement.

There was still so much more that Tom wanted to achieve, and to experience. I grieve for his loss of life, and my loss of him. Tom was my best friend, my soulmate. I adored him – I always will. I miss him more than I could ever describe.

We had been together for four years when, last October, Tom asked me to marry him. It was the most beautiful moment of my life. I said yes immediately, through tears of joy. We were deeply in love and blissfully happy together.

We had felt that the best was yet to come: our wedding, children, and a long and happy marriage. But it was all only ever to be a dream.

In a matter of seconds wedding plans and a future together had changed to funeral plans and a lifetime apart. I will never forget the complete confusion of Tom's three-year-old niece on the day of his funeral: one day being swung through the air and chased around the garden by her beloved Uncle Thomas; the next, there were no more games, there was no more laughter – only tears. As she sat quietly by his graveside, her little hands gripping hold of the edge, we watched her Uncle Thomas being gently lowered in a 'big box' into the ground. If there was anything left of my heart to break, it broke in that moment.

The pain is unlike anything I have ever experienced, and unlike anything I could ever have imagined. I feel as though Carty and Brown have ripped out my heart with their bare hands and torn it, very slowly, into pieces. Witnessing the pain that our families and friends are also suffering only adds to my own. The waves of devastation caused by Carty's and Brown's greed and bravado roll on and on.

There are no more tomorrows here for me and Tom, and all of our hopes and dreams have been brutally torn away. I just hope that there is something better for us on the other side.

In the meantime, just as hate and bitterness had no place in Tom's life, neither will they in his memory. I am determined to ensure, along with many others, that as much good as possible comes out of this horrific tragedy, so that I can say to Tom when I see him again, as I believe I will: 'That was the most agonising experience of my life, but everything that you worked so hard to achieve, and everything of you that you left behind was cherished and built upon to improve the lives of others in the way you would have wanted – and it was all done out of our great love for you.'

Wounds of the spirit

There are wounds of the spirit which never close, and are intended in God's mercy to bring us ever nearer to him, and to prevent us leaving him, by their very perpetuity. Such wounds, then, may almost be taken as a pledge, or at least as a ground for the humble trust, that God will give us the great gift of perseverance to the end... This is how I comfort myself in my own great bereavements.

John Henry Newman (1801–90)

Love in your sorrow

He is not in the least impatient with you for crying; no, nor for that deep sort of grief which would like to cry, but the tears will not come. Do not be in a hurry. He loves you *in* your sorrow. He is moved tenderly towards you because of your sorrow. He knows all about it in his own experience.

H. C. G. Moule (1841–1920),
late Bishop of Durham

We who are left

We who are left, how shall we look again
Happily on the sun or feel the rain,
Without remembering how they who went
Ungrudgingly, and spent
Their all for us, loved too the sun and rain?

A bird among the rain-wet lilac sings –
But we, how shall we turn to little things,
And listen to the birds and winds and streams

Made holy by their dreams,
Nor feel the heart-break in the heart of things?

Wilfred Gibson (1878–1962)

Thank God for them

Let us thank God for the years they were with us, for the gaiety and happiness, and the companionship and love they gave us. These are things that nothing can take away, they are ours to hold in our hearts and cherish all the days of our lives. Let us dwell on these things, and not on the sadness of a temporary farewell.

Author unknown

All is well

Death is nothing at all . . . I have only slipped away into the next room. I am I and you are you. Whatever we were to each other that we are still. Call me by my old familiar name, speak to me in the easy way which you always used. Put no difference in your tone; wear no forced air of solemnity or sorrow. Laugh as we always laughed at the little jokes we enjoyed together. Play, smile, think of me, pray for me. Let my name be ever the household word that it always was. Let it be spoken without effort, without the ghost of a shadow on it. Life means all that it ever meant. It is the same as it ever was; there is absolutely unbroken continuity. Why should I be out of mind because I am out of sight? I am waiting for you for an interval, somewhere very near, just around the corner. All is well.

Henry Scott Holland (1847–1918)

PRAYERS

So much together

Lord, all these years we were so close to one another, we did everything together, we seemed to know what each was feeling, without the need of words, and now she is gone. Every memory hurts . . . sometimes there comes a feeling that she is near, just out of sight. Sometimes I feel your reproach that to be so submerged in grief is not to notice that she is as eager to keep in touch with me, as I with her. O dear Lord, I pray out of a sore heart that it may be so, daring to believe that it can be so.

George Appleton (1902–93)

The grand encounter

Lord Christ,
Your life must touch my life,
Your words enliven,
Your look enhearten.
I need your presence in my desolation,
Your tears of sorrow for my consolation.
I need to meet you in my earthly time,
To know the beauty of your life in mine,
Then, at the end, uniquely face to face,
The grand encounter of your perfect grace.

David M. Owen

Single again

I'm single again, Lord,
for I have lost the companion of my journey,
and the love of my life.
And now I find myself in a strange place,
lost and alone.
I'm pining for her, longing to talk to her,
to put an arm around her, but she's gone,
and I'll never have her with me again.
There's an emptiness all around me –
the empty room, empty chair, empty bed.

I cook for myself, but don't enjoy it much –
not like it used to be when we were together,
and I would compliment her on a lovely meal.
I'm rock-bottom in my awful loneliness –
Please help me, Lord.

David M. Owen

The gift of tears

Lord, we give you thanks for the gift of tears:
For tears of grief, redeeming our mourning from despair;
For tears of anger, awakening our thirst for justice;
For tears of laughter, celebrating our joy in living.

May the light of Christ shining through our tears
Become the rainbow of your promise,
Shedding colours of your love's bright presence
In your grieving, struggling, laughing world.

Author unknown

God of all consolation

God of all consolation,
In your unending love and mercy for us
You turn the darkness of death
Into the dawn of new life.
Show compassion to your people in their sorrow.

Be our refuge and our strength
To lift us from the darkness of this grief
To the peace and light of your presence.

Your son, our Lord Jesus Christ,
By dying for us, conquered death
And by rising again, restored life.

May we then go forward eagerly to meet him,
And after our life on earth
Be reunited with our brothers and sisters
Where every tear will be wiped away.

Author unknown

For thy love's sake

Watch thou, O Lord, with those who wake, or watch, or weep tonight, and give thine angels charge over those who sleep. Tend thy sick ones, O Lord Christ; rest thy weary ones; bless thy dying ones; soothe thy suffering ones; pity thine afflicted ones; shield thy joyous ones, and all for thy love's sake.

St Augustine of Hippo (353–430)

I have to cry

I have to cry, Lord; I can't help it. But let not his/her death consume me: let not my crying be my dying, rather a necessary stage along the way to living again. In this way I shall honour him/her best, and give testimony to your restoring presence.

David M. Owen

A new finding

Lord, I've lost my wife in death, my dearest love, my very best friend, and in my loneliness I am grieving day and night. I say I have 'lost' her, but help me, Lord, to know that I have found her in a new way, deeper in my heart than ever I could have imagined, and growing ever more precious in my memory of her. May the lostness of her physical company, hurting as it is, be filled with the awareness of her spiritual presence around and within me. And may the faith I hold that tells me that you, in your great love, have found her a place in your eternal kingdom, and that we will find each other again and always be together, be my constant strength and hope.

David M. Owen

Comfort us who mourn

Eternal God,
Lord of life, conqueror of death,
our help in every time of trouble,
comfort us who mourn;
and give us grace, in the presence of death,
to worship you, the ever-living,
so that we may have sure hope of eternal life
and be enabled to put our whole trust
in your goodness and mercy;
through Jesus Christ our Lord.

A Book of Services and Prayers

11

Our living Lord

———◆◆◆———

In our earlier look at the New Testament's teaching on life after death (pages 6–18), we noted how the four Gospels climax their accounts of the life of Jesus with the news of his resurrection following his death by crucifixion. He had regarded his death as the necessary fulfilment of his divine purpose to give his life as 'a ransom for many', and he saw his death as a baptism symbolizing new life for all who believe. He expected his own resurrection, and several times repeated the prediction that he would rise again.

Although the Gospels conclude their records with this astounding news, it is anything but the end of the Jesus story. Rather it is the beginning of a whole new way of life, a new faith, as the apostles and others rejoiced in the great good news, and participated in spreading it far and wide.

And so across two thousand years, Christians have celebrated the triumph of that first Easter morning. Christ's resurrection has been the pinnacle and driving force, indeed the *raison d'être* and the central belief and inspiration for all his committed followers. Jesus told his disciples: 'Because I live, you too will live' (John 14.19 NEB), and to Martha he declared: 'I am the resurrection and I am life. If a man has faith in me, even though he die, he shall come to life' (John 11.25 NEB).

We owe the greatest debt to Jesus, not just for his wonderful love displayed on the cross and his rising from the dead, but also for what he has done to death itself. Yes, death does rob us of our one and only precious life – he knew that, and wept at the death of his friend Lazarus – and it is his wish that every one of us should live healthy and happy lives over many years. But, far from death being always the cruel destroyer, he has transformed it into a means of grace for a time when it is necessary, as it must be for all of us. Death for the believer is therefore not extinction but fulfilment, not a catastrophe but an accomplishment, and the gateway to a greater life. What God has prepared for those who love him rightly remains beyond our knowledge, but we can be sure it is the culmination of a process already begun. In fact, to be a follower of Christ here is to be in possession of it already, as the first letter of John reminds us: 'God has given us eternal life, and this life is found in his Son. He who possesses the Son possesses life' (1 John 5.11–12 REB).

Christians believe that Jesus not only passed through death but conquered it and gave it as a gift to us all, that he is the unique and stupendous hope by which we live our lives, and from which we draw consolation in our own times of sorrow.

REFLECTIONS

Christ rising in us

The death and resurrection of Christ draw near to us and touch us in the sacrament. The bread is broken – there Christ dies; we receive it as Christ alive – there is his resurrection. It is the typical expression of divine power to make something from nothing. God has made the world where no world was, and God makes life out of death. Such is the God with whom we have to do. We do not come to God for a little help, a little support to our own good intentions. We come to him for resurrection. God will not be asked for a little, he will be asked for all. We reckon ourselves dead, says St. Paul, that we may ask God for a resurrection, not of ourselves, but of Christ in us.

Austin Farrer (1906–68)

We shall be like him

'The Lord Jesus Christ . . . will transform our lowly bodies so that they will be like his glorious body' (Philippians 3.20–21). We look, not for a reassembling of our earthly body, but for a complete transformation of life: 'what we will be has not yet b'en made known. But we know that when he appears, we shall be like him, for we shall see him as he is' (1 John 3.2). We cannot yet see or even imagine the glorified body of Jesus, but we believe that we shall be like him, transfigured and redeemed by God. And this process begins even during earthly life: 'we, who with unveiled faces all reflect the Lord's glory, are being transformed into his likeness with ever-increasing glory' (2 Corinthians 3.18).

The New Testament teaching is that our earthly life is something like a growth from seed, or like a birth from the womb. What we do on earth is of eternal significance, for what will be built on in eternity is what we have begun on earth. But what we do on earth is not the end, for the evil will be transformed and the good fulfilled, as we share in the mind of God, which includes and reconciles all earthly experience, good and bad, into the divine life.

The resurrection of Jesus is the appearing in time of the transfigured future, a prototype of the glory of God that brings all creation into the divine life, and enables creatures to share in it.

Keith Ward

Sunset to dawn

Christ has turned all our sunsets into dawns.

Clement of Alexandria (*c*. 150–*c*. 215)

Out of the tomb

So Jesus was 'crucified, dead and buried'. No one, as far as we know, had ever survived that. The Roman way of condemnation, humiliation and death made sure of the end for its hapless victims.

Not so for Jesus. After the stark credal obituary Christians can hardly wait to declare, 'but on the third day he rose again from the dead', for so he did.

For the early witnesses of the resurrection – Mary Magdalene, the other women and the disciples and friends, it was a bewildering, yet exhilarating, experience – 'too good to be true', as we would say, but gradually the amazing truth became a reality as Jesus walked and talked with them and many others again before ascending to the Father.

He who went 'unto the cross' came 'out of the tomb', with all-important consequences for all generations since.

David M. Owen

My God gave me a morning (Mary Magdalene)

My God gave me a morning, at first a cheerless morning,
    for Christ my Lord was dead,
    and lay in death's cold grave;
    and I had come in grief
    his body to prepare,
    to do for him this final deed
    of solemn love and dignity.
My God gave me a morning, a mystifying morning,
    for empty was the tomb,
    and I was stunned with loss.
    Then, suddenly a voice,
    'Why weep your bitter tears,
    who is it that you sorely seek?'
    'I seek the Lord no longer here.'
My God gave me a morning, a bright and wondrous
      morning,
    for Christ before me stood
    and called me by my name.
    'Rabboni,' I replied,

'My Master and my Lord!'
And lowly kneeling at his feet
I clung to him with shameless zeal.
My God gave me a morning, a resurrection morning,
'Cling not to me,' he said,
'for I must now ascend,
and those I love must know,
and you must tell them so.'
I tell it proudly unto all
that Christ the Lord is living now!

David M. Owen

Jesus Lives

In light defeating darkness,
In wisdom conquering foolishness,
In trust overcoming fearfulness,
        Jesus Lives.

In strength coming to weakness,
In health rescuing from sickness,
In hope saving from despair,
        Jesus Lives.

In love victorious over hatred,
In forgiveness dispelling anger,
In glory dispersing drabness,
        Jesus Lives.

In joy growing from sorrow,
In life rising from death,
In God giving the victory,
        Jesus Lives.

He holds the keys of love
                of peace
He holds the keys of life
                of death

> He holds the keys of heaven
> of earth
> He holds the keys of now
> of eternity.

David Adam

On such a lovely morning

> In the sky
> The song of the skylark
> Greets the dawn.
> In the fields wet with dew
> The scent of the violets
> Fills the air.
> On such a lovely morning as this
> Surely on such a lovely morning as this
> Lord Jesus
> Came forth
> From the tomb.

Misuno Genzo (1937–84), a Japanese poet
and paraplegic who communicated with a
code based on movement of his eyelids:
translated by Marjorie Tunbridge

Belief in the Resurrection

Belief in the Resurrection is not an appendage to the Christian faith; it is the Christian faith.

We cannot begin to understand how it happened. The Gospels cannot explain the Resurrection; it is the Resurrection which alone explains the Gospels.

J. S. Whale (1896–1997)

Easter faith

It is the Easter faith, the faith in the risen and living Lord, which makes us able to meet life. For if we believe that Jesus Christ is risen and living, then we must believe that all life is lived in his presence, that we are literally never alone, that we are called upon to make no effort, to endure no sorrow, to face no temptation without him.

It is the Easter faith . . . which makes us able to meet death. It is the Easter faith that we have a friend and a companion who lived and who died and who is alive for ever more, who is the conqueror of death. The presence which is with us in life is with us in death and beyond.

William Barclay (1907–78)

Written promise

Our Lord has written the promise of the resurrection not in books alone, but in every leaf in springtime.

Martin Luther (1483–1546)

PRAYERS

Lord of life

O Lord of life, our Father and our Saviour,
    whose love will never cease,
      Help us, through every human bond releasing,
      to know your perfect peace.

O Living Lord, accept the life surrendered,
    our friend and loved-one here;
      Let every word and deed in life accomplished
      be now an offered prayer.

Life-giving Lord, whose death and resurrection
    is all our hope and gain,
      Gladly we trust, that with your Church Triumphant,
      we'll meet in you again.

David M. Owen, hymn for a funeral service
Suggested tune: Berwyn

Give us grace

Almighty God, give us grace that we may cast away the works of darkness, and put upon us the armour of light, now in the time of this mortal life, in which thy Son Jesus Christ came to visit us in great humility; that in the last day, when he shall come again in his glorious Majesty to judge both the quick and the dead, we may rise to the life immortal, through him who liveth and reigneth with thee and the Holy Ghost, now and ever. Amen.

Book of Common Prayer (1662)

For us who remain

> Almighty Saviour,
> Those who have died in faith
> have eternal joy in your presence.
> For us who remain, be with us
> in our sadness
> and turn our eyes to you.
> By your death once for all
> upon the cross,
> raise us to new life,
> give us victory over death,
> and confidence to look forward
> to your coming. Amen.

Pocket Words of Comfort

The gift of life

> Living Lord
> We celebrate your gift of life
> in the wonder of the universe,
> in the beauty of nature,
> and in every creature on earth.
>
> We celebrate your gift of life
> in our fellow human beings,

in the birth of a baby,
and the vitality of childhood and youth;
by those of ageing years,
and in the example of those who have lived
in love and service for others.

We celebrate your gift of life
wherever goodness, love, joy and hope
replace evil, hatred, sorrow and despair,
and whenever individuals and societies
reach out to those in need.

We celebrate your gift of life
which, through suffering, death and resurrection,
you bestowed on all mankind for ever;
and for the faithful preaching of the gospel
by your Church through the years,
and still today.

Living Lord,
we celebrate your gift of life.

David M. Owen

Not forsaken

Lord Jesus, we are told that when you were suffering on the cross
you even felt that God had forsaken you. So great was your pain.
Help me, as I go through my present anguish, to know that God
has not left me to cope alone, but that he is very close and help-
ing me to bear it. And as he helped you turn suffering and death
into victory, so enable me to win through, to the honour of your
name.

David M. Owen

Risen Jesus, living Jesus

Risen Jesus, living Jesus,
nothing could defeat your calling –

cruel words of sinful mind,
evil deeds of humankind;
cross that knew your dying breath,
tomb that held you firm in death.
Conquered is the cross that shamed you,
vanquished is the tomb that claimed you.
   Praise we offer, and thanksgiving,
   Jesus risen, Jesus living.

Risen Jesus, living Jesus,
nothing will defeat your purpose –
nothing through the coming years,
naught of human sins or fears;
on your love our hope depends,
yours the love that never ends.
You have shown your love by dying,
and by rising, death defying.
   Praise we offer, and thanksgiving,
   Jesus risen, Jesus living.

David M. Owen

12

Heaven awaits

―――◦‣◦―――

From the dawn of history humans have looked forward to a life after death. Stone Age people buried their dead with tools and cooking utensils. The death rituals of Ancient Egypt, Chinese ancestor worship, Hindu belief in the eternal soul or atma, Buddhism's eightfold journey toward Nirvana, Plato's teaching on immortality – all testify to immortal longings. Belief in the survival of the soul after physical death is a universal element in all religions. The funerary rites of their religion have always recognized that humans are more than animals to be cast away with no future, and have accorded each person due dignity on his or her departure.

Is it all wishful thinking, or rather, an inseparable part of our makeup and experience of earthly life? Where has the longing come from, and why should we be possessed of it unless there is a satisfactory accomplishment? Do we not glimpse eternity during our sojourn here, when, as the poet Wordsworth believed, 'we see into the heart of things'? There are times when we feel small and insignificant, but more often we know ourselves to be larger than life and born for a destiny beyond death, which alone can fulfil our unfulfilled potential and redress life's inequalities. Immanuel Kant said, 'Man's faculties, desires and earthly gifts reach far beyond earthly use.'

The writer to the Hebrews recognized every person's immortal longings, but spoke as a believer in Christ, whose resurrection is our gateway to life beyond death: 'Here we have no permanent home, but we are seekers after the city which is to come' (Hebrews 13.14 NEB). It is in Christ who died and rose again that our anticipation of the hereafter becomes most hopeful and exciting because, we believe, it will be a life with him in heaven. And since it is 'with him' it can only be a life of unsurpassed quality and pleasure.

In heaven we shall have unlimited opportunity to attain to what Paul calls 'mature manhood, measured by nothing less than the full stature of Christ' (Ephesians 4.13 NEB). And in heaven we shall 'see God'. This is known as the 'beatific vision', and derives from Revelation 22.3–4: 'The throne of God and of the Lamb will be there, and his servants shall worship him; they shall see him face to face' (NEB). These words are echoed in our Lord's beatitude, 'How blest are those whose hearts are pure; they shall see God' (Matthew 5.8 NEB).

REFLECTIONS

The goal

With God to find hopefulness
In the land beyond all stress,
In the place of gentleness,
Where He will your soul caress,
Where there is new liveliness,
Where the Father will you bless.

May the hills be gentle,
May the valleys be bright,
May the sun shine upon you,
May the moon in the night,
Until your pilgriming soul
Comes to its eternal goal.

David Adam

To eternity

Where does the journey end?
Beyond where you can see.

Where do the years end?
That's unknown to you or me.

Where does life end?
In love and eternity.

David Adam

Hope alive

Those who hope for no other life are dead even for this.
Johann Wolfgang von Goethe (1749–1832)

Eternal spring

Winter is on my head but eternal spring is in my heart. The nearer I approach the end, the plainer I hear around me the immortal symphonies of the world to come. For half a century I have been writing my thoughts in prose and verse; but I feel that I have not said one-thousandth part of what is in me. When I have gone down to the grave I shall have ended my day's work; but another day will begin the next morning. Life closes in the twilight but opens with the dawn.

Victor Hugo (1802–85)

The sea has another shore

The man of faith may face death as Columbus faced his first voyage from the shores of Spain. What lies beyond the seas he cannot tell: all his special expectations may be mistaken, but his insight into the clear meaning of present facts may persuade him beyond doubt that the sea has another shore.

H. E. Fosdick (1878–1969)

Where I live by sight

I have formerly lived by hear-say and faith, but now I go where I shall live by sight, and shall be with him in whose company I delight myself.

John Bunyan (1628–88)

He shall suffice me

Yea, through life, death, through sorrow and through
  sinning
He shall suffice me, for he hath sufficed;
Christ is the end, for Christ was the beginning,
Christ the beginning, for the end is Christ.

F. W. H. Myers (1843–1901)

PRAYERS

Prepare a place

We seem to give them back to you, O God, who gave them to us . . . Yet as you did not lose them in giving, so we do not lose them by their return. O lover of souls, you do not give as the world gives. What you give you do not take away; for what is yours is ours also if we are yours. And life is eternal and love is immortal; and death is only a horizon; and a horizon is nothing save the limit of our sight. Lift us up, strong son of God, that we may see more clearly; draw us closer to yourself that we may know ourselves to be nearer to our loved ones who are with you. And while you prepare a place for them, prepare us also for that happy place, that where you are we may be also for evermore. Amen.

Charles Henry Brent (1862–1929)

The gate of heaven

Bring us, O Lord God, at our last awakening into the house and gate of heaven, to enter into that gate and dwell in that house, where there shall be no darkness nor dazzling, but one equal light; no noise nor silence, but one equal music; no fears nor hopes, but one equal possession; no ends, nor beginnings, but one equal eternity; in the habitations of thy glory and dominion, world without end.

John Donne (1571–1631)

Heaven here and beyond

Lord Jesus Christ, who taught us to pray to God our Father in heaven, we give thanks for all that is heavenly around us to delight our senses, and for all good and caring people who make our world a better place. And while we appreciate your heavenly presence here on earth, lead our thoughts and confirm our faith in the greater kingdom of heaven that awaits us beyond this life when we shall behold your glory and worship you in wonder, love and praise.

David M. Owen

Shall I one day see thee?

O my God, shall I one day see thee? What sight can compare to that great sight? Shall I see the source of that grace which enlightens me, strengthens me, and consoles me? As I came from thee, as I am made through thee, so, O my God, may I at last return to thee, and be with thee for ever and ever.

John Henry Newman (1801–90)

Begin heaven on earth

O God of patience and consolation, grant we beseech thee that with free hearts we may love and serve thee and our brethren; and, having thus the mind of Christ, may begin heaven on earth, and exercise ourselves therein till that day when heaven, where love abideth, shall seem no strange habitation to us; for Jesus Christ's sake.

Christina Rossetti (1830–94)

In heaven to see thy face

Lord Jesus, give us grace
On earth to love thee more,
In heaven to see thy face,
And with thy saints adore.

William Bullock (1798–1874)
and Henry Williams Baker (1821–77)

13

Together for ever

I am ceaselessly grateful to have been blessed with a happy marriage of 45 years, and a wife whom I loved dearly and lost in death. As I look forward in faith to the hereafter I naturally hope that the love we had for each other in this life will continue even more splendidly in the next, for I cannot imagine complete happiness unless we are together.

Should we expect a continuation in the next life of the relationships we formed in this one? I believe so. We are reminded, of course, that when Jesus was asked about the after-life relationships of a woman who had been married seven times, 'Whose wife will she be?', he answered that at the resurrection 'men and women do not marry; they are like angels in heaven' (Mark 12.25 NEB). It was a cynical question from the Sadducees who, as we know, did not believe in the resurrection of the dead. Jesus' reply showed how inappropriate it is to think of human relationships in heaven in exactly the same way as we have known them here on earth. The resurrection ushers in a new order of living in which the old laws of physical life are transformed. Life in heaven is of a new dimension and hitherto unknown experience.

It is good to have this larger vision. However fulfilling are our earthly relationships, they are never perfect and are often hindered by obstacles and restricted by our impositions. The resurrection releases our limitations as we become completely part of an ever-growing community of love.

But does this mean that our close personal ties, as within

marriage, lose their intimacy as they dissipate in a general and all-embracing love for an innumerable company? Surely not. In heaven, while our love will be limitless, it will not be less than we have known on earth. Not less, but more. There our broken relationships will be mended, and the ties that bound us until severed by death will be rejoined and strengthened.

Charles Kingsley's wife is said to have erected over his grave a white marble cross with the inscription, 'We have loved; we love; we shall love', and above it, encircling a cross, the words, 'God is love'.

Our hope and trust lie in God's love. It is worth noting the full text of that supreme assertion: 'God is love, and whoever lives in love lives in union with God and God lives in union with him' (1 John 4.16 GNB). If, as we believe, he wills the love relationship of marriage, the bond between parents and their children, and those of our close friendships, what sort of God would he be to allow death to destroy them for ever, or to disallow their continuation in the next life he has prepared for us? Surely not the loving Father whom Jesus revealed to us. Why such emphasis in the Bible on the love of God for each of us and our obligation to love one another if love ends at death, or we fail to recognize our loved ones in the hereafter?

We say in the marriage service, 'Those whom God has joined together, let no man separate.' How much more will God see to it that the bonds we have known, not just in marriage, but between us and all who are so dear to us, remain intact? Paul, in his magnificent 'Hymn of Love' (1 Corinthians 13), said that love, alongside faith and hope, lasts for ever, stressing that love, being the greatest, 'will never come to an end'.

REFLECTIONS

For ever and always

'Death' does not mean the end of all life, but actually, on the contrary, a birth, a passing over into a new life, a glorious and everlasting life. Hence death is not a fearful thing. It is the separation that is hard, and heavy to bear. But it becomes less hard and less heavy to bear when we remain mindful that we are indeed not parting for ever, but *only for a time* – as for a journey – in order afterwards to meet again *for ever and always* in a life that is infinitely more beautiful than the present one, and that then *there will be no end* of our being together. Remember all this and your burden will surely become lighter.

Alexander Schmorell

Life in the Lord

Those who live in the Lord never see each other for the last time.

A proverb

Unbreakable love

I want to meet again those I have known and loved, who before they 'died' helped me by their friendship and encouragement. If God is love as Jesus taught, then love is eternal, and a relationship of love cannot be broken by physical death.

George Appleton (1902–93)

With our loved ones

I love thee with a love I seemed to lose
With my lost saints – I love thee with the breath,
Smiles, tears, of all my life! – and, if God choose,
I shall but love thee better after death.

Elizabeth Barrett Browning (1806–61)

Together always

You were born together and together you shall be for
    evermore;
You shall be together when the white wings of death
    scatter your days,

Aye, you shall be together even in the silent memory of God.

Kahlil Gibran (1883–1931)

PRAYERS

We give thanks

We give you thanks, gracious Father, for our loved ones who meant so much to us in this life. Comfort our loss of them by the faith that tells us they are safe and happy in your presence, and by the hope that awaits the unspeakable pleasure of being united with them when we depart this life.

David M. Owen

For those whom we love

O Father of all, we pray to thee for those whom we love, but see no longer. Grant them thy peace; let light perpetual shine upon them; and in thy loving wisdom and almighty power work in them the good purpose of thy perfect will; through Jesus Christ our Lord. Amen.

Proposed Prayer Book (1928)

Inspired by their example

Almighty God, we beseech thee that, inspired by the example of thy saints, we may run with patience the race that is set before us, looking unto Jesus, the author and finisher of our faith; so that, when this mortal life is ended, we may be gathered with those whom we have loved, in the kingdom of thy glory, where there shall be no more death, neither sorrow nor crying, neither shall there be any more pain, for the former things are passed away; through Jesus Christ our Lord, Amen.

A Book of Services and Prayers

14

The eternal company

A clergyman returned home from an early morning church service at which there had been only six communicants. His wife expressed sadness that so few had attended, but he was not disappointed: 'True, there were only six that we could see, but when we prayed, "Therefore with angels and archangels, and with all the company of heaven, we laud and magnify thy holy name", I was reminded of all the others.'

All Saints' Day on 1 November is a reminder each year of 'all the others' – the countless number of 'saints, apostles, prophets, martyrs' who make up the Church redeemed and triumphant in heaven.

In his vision of that Church, John, the writer of the Book of Revelation, told of a crowd, too large to be counted, standing before God and offering their worship (7.9–10). In remembering the ever-expanding company of the faithful in heaven, and rejoicing in the spiritual fellowship of the Communion of the Saints, we realize how truly great the Church is.

The day following All Saints' is All Souls', set aside for the commemoration of the faithful departed. It is very much a personal festival when we recall and give thanks for those whom we have 'loved and lost awhile', but who too are part of the Church Triumphant in heaven. It's an occasion for everyone, for all of us who know the pain of parting brought about by the death of loved ones.

We don't, of course, have to wait for just one or two days in the year on which to remember and hold communion with them; they and we are part of each other at all times, bonded together in the love of God in which prayer for each other is a lifeline. In fact, there is no need for us to attempt any other contact with them – prayer alone, within the orbit of God's love, is sufficient.

REFLECTIONS

One family, one Church

Let saints below in concert sing
With those to glory gone;
For all the servants of our King
In earth and heaven are one.

One family we dwell in Him,
One Church, above, beneath,
Though now divided by the stream,
The narrow stream of death.

Charles Wesley (1707–88)

Joined in prayer

The saints, because they are closer to God now than when they were on earth, share even more intimately in his work. Part of that work is interceding for people according to Christ's will. We can, if we want, ask for the prayers of the saints in general or one saint in particular. We have friends on earth and sometimes we ask one of them to pray for us. We also have friends in heaven and it is just as natural to ask them to pray for us. It no more takes away from the centrality of Christ and his grace than asking an earthly friend to pray for us. All prayer, whether on earth or in heaven, is Christ praying in and through us.

It is just as natural to pray for the departed. More often than now happens, our prayers should express thanks. We should remember with gratitude particular aspects of the life and character of someone we have loved and give thanks to God for them. But this prayer can also include the request that the loved one be drawn ever deeper into God. The traditional words, 'Rest eternal grant unto them, O Lord. Let light perpetual shine upon them', have a never fading truth and beauty.

Richard Harries

A crossing the world

They that love beyond the world cannot be separated by it. Death is but a crossing the world, as friends do the seas; they live in one another still.

William Penn (1644–1718)

One in Christ

Each human being belongs not only to that part of humanity which, living on earth at the moment, stands before God in prayer and labour, for the present generation is only a page in the book of life. In God and in his church there is no difference between living and dead, and all are one in the love of the Father. Even the generations yet to be born are part of this one divine humanity.

Sergius Bulgakov (1871–1944)

PRAYERS

With countless others

Eternal Lord, whilst none of us can fully appreciate the splendour of heaven during our earthly journey, still, fill us with the spirit of wonder as we contemplate life together with countless others in one great communion and unbroken fellowship. Help us, while we live in this world, to look forward in faith to being part of that eternal company who love one another and ceaselessly glorify your holy name.

David M. Owen

Remember our brothers and sisters

Lord, remember in mercy your Church throughout the world; make all its members to grow in love for you and for one another.

Remember our brothers and sisters who have gone to their rest in the hope of the resurrection to eternal life; and bring us with them into the light of your presence, that in union with all your saints we may give you glory for ever, through your Son Jesus Christ our Lord.

Contemporary Parish Prayers

United to thyself

O Lord our God, from whom neither life nor death can separate those who trust in thy love, and whose love holds in its embrace thy children in this world and the next; so unite us to thyself that in fellowship with thee we may always be united to our loved ones whether here or there; give us courage, constancy and hope; through him who died and was buried and rose again for us, Jesus Christ our Lord.

William Temple (1881–1944)

The unseen cloud of witnesses

Eternal God, help us always to remember the great unseen cloud of witnesses round about us. When in danger, give us their courage and when in difficulty, their perseverance; so that we too may be faithful until we rejoice with all the saints in your eternal kingdom, through Jesus Christ our Lord. Amen.

William Hampson

Sources and acknowledgements

1 Death and the life after: What the Bible teaches

'Through the scriptures' from *New Every Morning*, ed. Frank Colquhoun (BBC, 1973).

Henry Williams Baker, 'Word of consolation', verses 1 and 5 of the hymn 'Lord, thy word abideth'.

Leslie D. Weatherhead, 'Our thanks for the Bible' (extract) from Tony Castle, *The Hodder Book of Christian Prayers* (Hodder, 1986). Reproduced by permission of Hodder and Stoughton Limited.

Jamie Wallace, 'Lord of all hopefulness' from Tony Castle, *The Hodder Book of Christian Prayers* (Hodder, 1986). Reproduced by permission of Hodder and Stoughton Limited.

2 The concept of the soul

Richard Harries, 'More than our physical parts' from *Being a Christian* (Mowbray, 1981).

John Polkinghorne, 'The real me' from *Quark, Chaos and Christianity* (SPCK, 1994).

Cardinal John Heenan, 'Immortal soul' from 'Only one answer makes sense' in *Is There a Life after Death?* (Arthur James, 1960).

Leslie D. Weatherhead, 'The inviolate soul' from *Time for God* (Lutterworth Press, 1967).

Dr James Casson, 'Survival of the spirit' from *Facing Bereavement* (Highland Books, 1988).

John Cole, 'Like a baby in the womb', © *The Times*, London, 15 February 1986.

Jan van Ruysbroeck, 'God in the soul' from *The Wisdom of the Saints*, ed. Jill Haak Adels (Oxford University Press, 1987).

Eric Milner-White, 'Unshackle my soul' from *My God, My Glory* (SPCK, 1967).

A. J. Cronin, 'Kingdom of the soul', quoted in a sermon by Charles Copenhauer, *The Expository Times*, March 1972, p. 179.

Charles Duthie, 'The soul's march', *The British Weekly*, 22 August 1968.

Michael Mayne, 'As at Tenebrae . . .' from *The Enduring Melody* (Darton, Longman & Todd, 2006). Quoted in *Church Times*, 10 November 2006.

'My soul, thy gift' from *The Great Mystery of Life Hereafter* (Hodder & Stoughton, 1957).

Joseph Hall, 'Prepare my soul' from Tony Castle, *The Hodder Book of Christian Prayers* (Hodder, 1986). Reproduced by permission of Hodder and Stoughton Limited.

3 Death no stranger

Christmas Humphreys, 'But life is immortal' from *The Great Mystery of Life Hereafter* (Hodder & Stoughton, 1957).

C. S. Lewis, 'Death does matter' from *A Grief Observed* (Faber & Faber, 1961).

John Donne, 'Involved in mankind' from *Devotions upon Emergent Occasions*, Meditation XVII.

'Death in life' from 'The burial of the dead', *Book of Common Prayer* (1662).

George Appleton, 'Help for those who suffer' from *Acts of Devotion* (SPCK, 1963).

4 Fear and faith

Franklin D. Roosevelt, 'Fear itself' from his First Inaugural Address, 1933.

'Fear so great', quoted in *Times 2*, © *The Times*, London, 22 February 2006.

Epictetus, 'Fearing the pain' from *Discourses*.

Bel Mooney, 'If you worry', *Times 2*, © *The Times*, London, 22 February 2006.

Rabindranath Tagore, 'I shall love death as well'.

Leslie D. Weatherhead, 'Jesus in the Garden' from *Psychology and Life* (Hodder & Stoughton, 1934).

Thomas Ken, 'To live and die', verse 3 of the hymn 'Glory to thee, my God, this night'.

Graham Smith, 'Death – my fears' from *Church Times*, 18 April 1980.

'Made for life' from Common Worship: Pastoral Services, *Pocket Words of Comfort* (Church House Publishing, 2004). © The Archbishops' Council 2004. Reproduced with permission.

James M. Todd, 'In whom is all our hope' from *Contemporary Parish Prayers*, ed. F. Colquhoun (Hodder & Stoughton, 1975).

The prayer 'Lighten our darkness Lord, we pray' from *The Alternative Service Book (1980)* is copyright © The central Board of Finance of the Church of England, 1980; The Archbishops' Council 1999 and is reproduced by permission.

Michael Hollings and Etta Gullick, 'Lord, I'm afraid' from *The Shade of his Hand* (McCrimmon Publishing Co. Ltd, 1973).

5 This life in preparation

Basil Hume, 'The moment of ecstasy' and 'One day I shall die' from *To Be a Pilgrim* (SPCK, 1984).

John Bunyan, 'If a man would live well' from *The Pilgrim's Progress*.

John Polkinghorne, 'Unto our destiny' from *Quarks, Chaos and Christianity* (SPCK, 1994).

Norman Pittenger, 'Life – a dying', *The British Weekly*, 29 November 1974.

Malcolm Muggeridge, 'Part of a larger pattern' from *Jesus Rediscovered* (Collins/Fontana, 1969).

Kahlil Gibran, 'For life and death are one' from *The Prophet* (Heinemann, 1926).

John Cole, 'The lesson from nature' from 'The meaning of death', © *The Times*, London, 15 February 1986.

John Henry Newman, 'And our work is done', an arrangement of a prayer by Lancelot Andrewes (1555–1626).

6 Too soon to die

Jane Davies, 'Sarah, aged seven' from *The Price of Loving* (Mowbray, 1981).

Arlene Stamy, 'Empty places'. Source unknown.

Marjorie Pizer, 'Lament' from *To You the Living: Poems of Bereavement and Loss* (Pinchgut Press, 6 Oaks Avenue, Cremorne, Sydney 2090, Australia, 1981).

Mary Yarnell, 'Too soon' from *Poems and Readings for Funerals*, ed. Julia Watson (Penguin, 2004). Copyright Mary Yarnell 2004. Reprinted by kind permission of Jonathan Clowes Ltd, London, on behalf of Julia Watson.

Alfred, Lord Tennyson, 'In God's completion' from *In Memoriam*.

David M. Owen, 'The widow of Nain' from *Jesus Encounter* (David M. Owen, 2006).

Richard Harries, 'Further stages of growth' from *Being a Christian* (Mowbray, 1981).

Viktor Frankl, 'The unfinisheds' from *Man's Search for Meaning* (Hodder, 1964).

Erich Fromm, 'Without having lived' from *Man for Himself* (Rinehart, 1947).

Buz Kohan, sung by Michael Jackson, 'Gone Too Soon' from the Compassionate Friends Poetry Corner.

'The Cord' from the Compassionate Friends Poetry Corner.

Joint Liturgical Group, 'So many hopes' and 'Aching hearts' from *Funeral Services of the Christian Churches in England* (SCM-Canterbury Press, 2002).

'Comfort this family' from *A New Zealand Prayer Book* (HarperCollins, 1989).

Fred Pratt Green, 'Lord Jesus, take this child'. Reproduced by permission of Stainer & Bell Ltd.

The Guild of Health, 'Sorrowing hearts' from Michael Hollings and Etta Gullick, *The Shade of his Hand* (McCrimmon Publishing Co. Ltd, 1973).

7 Unable to bear it

Suicide Prevention Centre, 'Expression of distress' from their 'Manual for Handling Telephone Calls', quoted by Howard Clinebell, *The Expository Times*, August 1966.

Carol Midgley, 'Then someone cared' from 'Young and Desperate', *Times 2*, 26 June 2007.

Marjorie Pizer, 'The existence of love', from *To You the Living: Poems of Bereavement and Loss* (Pinchgut Press, 6 Oaks Avenue, Cremorne, Sydney 2090, Australia, 1981).

Neville Smith, 'For those who despair' from *Prayers for People in Hospital* (Oxford University Press, 1994). By permission of Oxford University Press.

Michael Hollings and Etta Gullick, 'But she could not pull out of it' and 'You alone know what he suffered' from *The Shade of his Hand* (McCrimmon Publishing Co. Ltd, 1973).

Simon H. Baynes, 'Come unto me' from 'Meditation and prayer for those tempted to commit suicide', in *Prayers for Today's Church*.

Used by permission of Kingsway Publications, Lottbridge Drove, Eastbourne.

'Christ my helper' from *Prayer Fellowship Handbook 1972* (United Reformed Church).

8 Coping with disaster

Michael Mayne, 'To live in hope' from *The Enduring Melody* (Darton, Longman & Todd, 2006). Quoted in *Church Times*, 10 November 2006.

Frances Bridger, 'Ground Zero', *Church Times*, 3 November 2006.

C. R. North, 'What sort of world?' from *The Expository Times*, June 1967, p. 278.

J. B. Phillips, 'No intervention' from *God Our Contemporary* (Hodder & Stoughton, 1960).

Henry Francis Lyte, 'To God we cried' from the hymn 'Whom should we love like thee?'

David H. C. Read, 'God in the midst' from *The Expository Times*, March 1965, pp. 193–4.

Joint Liturgical Group, 'Following a natural disaster' and 'Following a disaster arising from human error or accident' from *Funeral Services of the Christian Churches in England* (SCM-Canterbury Press, 2002).

Malcolm Muggeridge, *Jesus Rediscovered* (Collins Fontana, 1969). Reproduced with permission.

'Why, Lord?' from *Prayer Fellowship Handbook 1978* (United Reformed Church).

Michel Quoist, 'The hospital' from *Prayers of Life* (Gill & Macmillan, Dublin, 1963). Reproduced with permission.

9 The cost of war

Neil Oliver, 'Known unto God' and 'The Unknown Warrior' from *Not Forgotten* (Hodder & Stoughton, 2005). Reproduced by permission of Headline Publishing Group Limited.

The Prince of Wales, 'Courage in duty' from his Foreward to Michael Ashcroft, *Victoria Cross Heroes* (Headline, 2006). Reproduced by permission of Headline Publishing Group Limited.

Sean O'Neill, 'A widow's wreath', © *The Times*, London, 13 November 2006.

Walter Rookes, 'The family', *Times 2*, © *The Times*, London, 27 October 2006.

Siegfried Sassoon, 'Jesus, make it stop' from 'Attack' in *Collected Poems 1908–1956* (Faber & Faber, 1984), © Siegfried Sassoon by kind permission of the Estate of George Sassoon.

Rachel Mann, 'Prayer: sacred and profane', *Church Times*, 10 November 2006.

Siegfried Sassoon, 'Suicide in the trenches' from *Collected Poems 1908–1956* (Faber & Faber, 1984), © Siegfried Sassoon by kind permission of the Estate of George Sassoon.

Wilfred Owen, 'What, for those who die?' from 'Anthem for Doomed Youth'.

Michael Davis, 'They died for us' from 'Thoughts on Remembrance Sunday', *Words For Worship*, ed. Christopher Campling and Michael Davis (Edward Arnold, 1969).

Laurence Binyon, 'We will remember them' from 'For the fallen'.

Sue Ryder and Leonard Cheshire, 'Honouring those who died' from *Pocket Prayers* (Church House Publishing, 2004). © The Archbishops' Council 2004. Reproduced by permission.

David M. Owen, 'From war to peace' from *Priory Praise* (Priory Publishing, 1986).

Frank Colquhoun, 'For all who suffer' (adapted) from *Contemporary Parish Prayers*, ed. F. Colquhoun (Hodder & Stoughton, 1975). Reproduced by permission of Hodder and Stoughton Limited.

10 Solace in grief

Colin Murray Parkes, 'Growing stronger' from *Bereavement* (Penguin, 1975).

Marjorie Pizer, 'Rebirth' from *To You the Living: Poems of Bereavement and Loss* (Pinchgut Press, 6 Oaks Avenue, Cremorne, Sydney 2090, Australia, 1981).

Martin Israel, 'Towards meaningfulness' from *Living Alone* (SPCK, 1982).

Simon Stephens, 'The sharing of grief'.

Neil Oliver, 'Healing time' from *Not Forgotten* (Hodder & Stoughton, 2005). Reproduced by permission of Headline Publishing Group Limited.

Joyce Grenfell, 'Life goes on'. 'If I should go before the rest of you' (copyright © The Joyce Grenfell Memorial Trust, 1980) is reproduced by permission of Sheil Land Associates Ltd on behalf of The Estate of Joyce Grenfell.

C. Day Lewis, 'Living in laughter' from 'A time to dance' in *The Complete Poems of C. Day Lewis* (Sinclair-Stevenson, 1992). Copyright The Estate of C. Day Lewis. Reprinted by permission of The Random House Group Ltd.

C. J. Lewis, 'The feel of grief' from *A Grief Observed* (Faber & Faber, 1961).

Marcel Proust, 'As when they were alive' from *In Search of Lost Time*, translated by C. K. Scott Moncrieff, published by Chatto & Windus. Reprinted by permission of The Random House Group Ltd.

Adele Eastman, 'A brutal and terrible loss', © *The Times*, London, 29 November 2006. Reproduced by permission. Tom's parents, Adele and Linklaters LLP have established the Tom ap Rhys Price Memorial Trust, whose goals are to provide training opportunities to individuals who might not otherwise have access to them, and to tackle the root causes of violent street crime. Details of the trust's work can be found at <www.tomaprhyspryce.com>.

Wilfred Gibson, 'We who are left' from *Collected Poems 1905–1925* (Pan Macmillan). Copyright © W. W. Gibson, 1926.

Henry Scott Holland, 'All is well', verses 4–5 of the hymn 'Grant us thy light' (adapted).

George Appleton, 'So much together', from *Pocket Words of Comfort*, compiled by Christopher Herbert (Church House Publishing, 2004).

David M. Owen, 'The grand encounter' from *Jesus Encounter* (David M. Owen, 2006).

'Comfort us who mourn' from *A Book of Services and Prayers* (Independent Press, 1959). Reproduced by permission of the United Reformed Church.

11 Our living lord

Austin Farrer, 'Christ rising in us' from *Pocket Words of Comfort* (Church House Publishing, 2004). © The Archbishops' Council 2004.

Keith Ward, 'We shall be like him' from *What the Bible Really Teaches* (SPCK, 2004).

David Adam, 'Jesus Lives' from *Tides and Seasons* (Triangle, 1989).

Misuno Genzo, 'On such a lovely morning', *The Japanese Christian Quarterly* (Summer 1984).

J. S. Whale, 'Belief in the Resurrection', *Christian Doctrine* (Collins/Fontana, 1941).

William Barclay, 'Easter faith', *The British Weekly*, February 1964.

David M. Owen, 'Lord of life', from *Priory Praise* (Priory Publishing, 1986).

'For us who remain' from Common Worship: Pastoral Services in *Pocket Words of Comfort* (Church House Publishing, 2004). © The Archbishops' Council 2004.

12 Heaven awaits

David Adam, 'The goal' and 'To eternity' from *Tides and Seasons* (Triangle, 1989).

H. E. Fosdick, 'The sea has another shore' from *Short Prayers for the Long Day*, ed. Giles and Melville Harcourt (Collins, 1978).

F. W. H. Myers, 'He shall suffice me', verse 4 of the hymn 'Hark what a sound'.

William Bullock and Henry Williams Baker, 'In heaven to see thy face', verse 5 of the hymn 'We love the place, O God'.

13 Together for ever

Alexander Schmorell, 'For ever and always' from a letter to his parents before his execution by the Nazis in May 1943.

George Appleton, 'Unbreakable love', *Daily Telegraph*.

Elizabeth Barrett Browning, 'With our loved ones' from *Sonnets from the Portuguese*.

Kahlil Gibran, 'Together always' from *The Prophet* (Heinemann, 1926).

'Inspired by their example' from *A Book of Services and Prayers* (Independent Press, 1959). Reproduced by permission of the United Reformed Church.

The *Proposed Prayer Book* (1928), from *Pocket Words of Comfort*, compiled by Christopher Herbert (Church House Publishing, 2004).

14 The eternal company

Charles Wesley, 'One family, one Church', verses 2 and 3 of the hymn 'Come, let us join our friends above'.

Richard Harries, 'Joined in prayer' from *Being a Christian* (Mowbray, 1981).

'Remember our brothers and sisters', adapted from a Roman Catholic requiem in *Contemporary Parish Prayers*, ed. F. Colquhoun (Hodder & Stoughton, 1975). Reproduced by permission of Hodder and Stoughton Limited.